MONEY
and
SPIRIT

MONEY
and
SPIRIT

Creating a New Consciousness in Making and Managing Your Money

by Frederick S. Brown

A.R.E. Press • Virginia Beach • Virginia

A.R.E. Press
Sixty-Eighth & Atlantic Avenue
P.O. Box 656
Virginia Beach, VA 23451-0656

Library of Congress Cataloging-in-Publication Data
Brown, Frederick S., 1938-
    Money and spirit : creating a new consciousness in making
and managing your money / by Frederick S. Brown.
        p.   cm.
    Includes bibliographical references.
    ISBN 0-87604-331-7
    1. Finance, Personal. 2. Finance, Personal—Religious as-
pects. I. Title.
HG179.B7464   1995
332.024—dc20   94-37665

AUTHOR'S NOTE:
Although the cases in this book are based on ones in my files, the
characters, names, and events are fictitious.

Cover design by Richard Boyle

Dedication

I dedicate this book to my wife, Leila, and my clients and students without whom this book would never have materialized.

Table of Contents

Introduction

The Money and Spirit Connection

WHEN I was young, money had an enormous power over me. My father was a stockbroker, and his moods rose and fell with the ups and downs of the stock market. Since he was a product of the Depression, he worried a great deal about money and instilled me with his concern.

He was a sensitive man who was never completely at ease with the hard realities of business. One of his most endearing qualities was his openness, and during my growing-up years he gave the family a steady commentary of the traumas he went through on Wall Street. Although I'm sure he was unaware of it, his recitals amplified my financial anxieties and persuaded me to believe that money was my only true source of security.

When my turn came to follow in my father's footsteps, I was a Wall Street disciple, but as I watched my father's career ebb and his health fail, I began to think that chasing dollars might not be the be-all and end-all of life.

I could see that as much as my father wanted to, he couldn't reconcile the greed ethic of his business with his staunch Presbyterian ethic, and the effort to live with them both played a major role in destroying his nerves and perpetuating a death-inducing asthmatic condition.

After ten years of suffering and hundreds of hours on the respirator, my father collapsed and so did whatever faith I had left in the power of money.

Fortunately into my void came information about Edgar Cayce,[1] an extraordinary individual who without any medical experience could diagnose illnesses, prescribe cures, and give meaningful life readings in a trance state. This man, given little more than an eighth-grade education, was able, through his faith and his intense desire to serve others, to tap into a higher source of spiritual knowledge. Reading his cases and his correspondence with his patients convinced me of the truth of his words.

The Cayce material inspired me to learn as much as I could about my spiritual resources from the Bible, the *Bhagavad Gita*, Carl Jung, Emmanuel, Ram Dass, the Quakers, and many others. Their teachings helped me discover that my real search in life was for inner peace and that my strength and power came from within myself and not from the material world.

Their wisdom changed my ideas about money. Money was no longer just a commodity for gaining material security, but a precious energy that I could use to help me find this peace.

Shortly after my father's death, I began to realize that making people richer in the stock market did not necessarily enrich their lives, and I gave up being an investment advisor and became a personal financial consultant, writer, and teacher.

Using my sessions and classrooms as a laboratory, I explored the nature of people's attitudes toward managing money. I soon discovered how much they disliked dealing with their checkbooks, taxes, insurance, and other finances. Many felt so threatened by them they avoided the most basic steps of managing, like keeping track of their bank balances or paying their bills on time.

When I looked into the reasons for these fears, I found a chronicle of family money issues. These issues had overwhelmed them and stifled their will to manage. Through trial and error I learned that the most effective way to change people's negative attitudes is to have them examine their fears and finances in light of their higher purposes. When they see how their past anxieties sabotage these purposes and how their highest pattern of behavior and financial facts can guide them to right decision making, they are more than willing to take charge of their money.

For me this is the most exciting part of being a consultant, because the moment they make that money and spirit connection, a new light enters their eyes and the tension leaves their body. Suddenly I feel I'm in the presence of their true spirit. When this happens, I know they can work out solutions to their problems for I see they are no longer stymied by their own fears.

In *Money and Spirit* I share my approach with you. I hope it will help you overcome your management anxieties and give you the peace of mind you deserve.

1

The Fears
of Managing Money

ONE DAY in my class on "Money and Spirit" a student named Maria shared her feelings about managing money in a brief report. Here is what she said:

> "Money haunts me. It is the demon that frightens me. Every time I struggle to make a money-related decision, I think I want to live without money because I hate it. At the same time I wish I had millions of dollars so that I wouldn't have to worry about it. Thinking of it now makes me want to scream: I HATE MONEY!"

We were all touched by Maria's words as they reminded us of the spiritual burdens that money managing can inflict on us.

After class I offered to help Maria deal with her financial problems. She hesitated to accept my offer, and I could see from the expression on her face that she was afraid of what it might entail.

I quickly assured her that I wouldn't make her do more than she was able. I told her candidly that I didn't enjoy managing my money any more than she did hers and wouldn't burden her with guilt, judgments, or impossible tasks. All I would ask her to do was to let me help her look at her fears and try to make some sense of them.

Maria still balked, and I can remember the excuses she gave me as they were the litany I had heard from so many people.

"I'll never understand money," she said. "My facts are meaningless"; "I don't deserve to have money"; "I never have enough"; "I have too little to manage"; "My financial position isn't worth looking at"; and the most devastating one of all, *"I just can't do it!"*

I knew these excuses were symptomatic of someone caught up in anxiety, and I didn't let them deter me. After further persuasion, Maria agreed to see me, and we set up our first session the following week.

Going home that day I couldn't get Maria's report out of my mind. Her attitude conveyed the same negativity and fear that I believed plagued most people. I was sure it was this attitude that prevented people from managing their money effectively.

Although I wasn't aware of it at the time, I think in the back of my mind was the idea of using Maria's story as a focal point for this book. In any case that is what eventually happened.

Before we get into her case, however, we need to have an understanding of the nature of Maria's and our anxieties so that we can see what we are up against.

My counseling has taught me that these anxieties are inextricably connected to our self-doubts and fear for survival. Many of us are terrified of handling our money because we don't believe we can do it well, and to do it wrong would jeopardize our very existence.

On a deeper level, we know that money is not the source of life, but our egos don't, and they drive us to act as if it were. They imprison us in self-doubts and prevent us from tapping into the true source of our management power, our spirit.

To illustrate, I was reminded of the ordeal my wife Leila and I underwent when we tried to sell our house in Maine. We were moving to New Mexico and had purchased a home there.

Now you might think that I, being a personal financial consultant, would have had enough sense to get the proper appraisal to determine the fair price. Yet I didn't. I let myself get caught up in the broker's enthusiasm and priced the Maine house according to the highest price he thought he could get.

The old adage that greed never prevails came true again. We had to suffer through nine months of waiting before the house sold and, when it did, the amount was substantially below our original offering price, but at a price that gave us just what we needed to cover the cost of our home in New Mexico.

Since I believe that we were meant to move there, I'm sure if we had priced the Maine house according to the cost of the home in New Mexico, we would not have had to suffer through those months of false bids and maintenance bills.

In retrospect I realize we acted the way we did because all I could hear was my protectionist, competitive ego shouting at us to get the highest price instead of the still, small voice of spirit saying: Ask for what you need and it will be given.

Why is the selfish, insecure voice the one we listen to

most often? The answer is self-evident. Our own self-doubts program us to hear the fearful sounds that come from our family, personal experience, and society. These outside voices are very persuasive, and to resist them we need to look at how they lead us astray.

THE FAMILY

The most pervasive source of our financial anxieties is the family. From the moment we enter the womb we become a part of our family's financial struggle and the financial anxieties that go along with it.

To come to terms with our anxieties we need to look at our own family's financial history and learn how we have been influenced by it. Then we need to work on getting rid of any of the fearful attitudes we've inherited.

One of the most challenging histories I know of came from a student named Ellen. Here is her report:

ELLEN'S REPORT

"My father was a professional officer in the army. My mother was a homemaker and mother of six children. I am the eldest. Money to my parents represented status, intelligence, good breeding, social standing, and privilege. We were a Catholic upper-middle-class family.

"Money was used as a source of control, manipulation, and power. If I was in agreement with my parents, money was available to me in a limited way. If I wasn't, money was withheld. As I was the black sheep of the family, I got nothing I deserved or asked for.

"We lived in an autocratic home. I never had a say in how money would be spent, and my parents never discussed money with me although they fought about it constantly.

"Since my father thought family members should not be allowed to work, I was not allowed to have jobs as an adolescent and teen-ager outside the home or family business and was rarely paid for my services.

"I was not allowed to choose my own style of clothing, hair, books, music, art film, friends, etc., or to purchase anything without permission. The things I loved were equated with decadence and nonproductivity.

"We were expected to be self-sufficient upon graduating from college (we were all expected to go), and my father stated that his responsibility for us ended at that point. I was emotionally and financially unprepared for 'leaving the nest,' and now I am forty-seven and have no assets, home insurance, property, or savings.

"One of the heaviest learning experiences was having my son and being destitute. I finally had to face the fact that money was the problem. The discrepancy between the material wealth I grew up in and the poverty I live in has been difficult. I want to give us items, go places, do things; but we can't. Money can give wonderful pleasures and comfort if obtained gracefully and used well."

*   *   *

The financial control of Ellen by her family is an extreme example of what can happen when parents project their fears onto their children. In their attempt to control their daughter's spending, Ellen's parents were trying to cope with the common parental belief that kids are naturally irresponsible with money. From the beginning of a child's financial life, parents start teaching management with caveats or, as in Ellen's case, rigid financial rules which, unless used compassionately, become fear-inducing proclamations that attack the child's self-worth.

We all remember those parental exclamations at our requests for money:

"Do you want to put me in the poor house?"
"Do you think I'm made of money?"
"Money doesn't grow on trees."
"We're not made of money, you know!"
"How can you think you deserve more money when you spend it the way you do?"
"If you ask me for money one more time, I'll disinherit you."
"You are going to nickel-and-dime me to death."
"Do you think you're really worth it?"

These kinds of responses are not necessarily meant to be hurtful. They're simply a projection of the parents' own financial frustrations. However, the anxiety they engender in a child can last a lifetime.

The warnings, rules, and responses are just the beginning of the fear-induced pattern of thinking about money that usually pervades the growing-up scene. The continual financial fighting that Ellen experienced is a normal hazard in most families and a major reason why children have a negative attitude toward money.

The uneasy feelings created by these arguments are compounded when parents like Ellen's refuse to discuss their finances openly. For without sufficient explanations, children have no basis for understanding the reasons for the brouhahas.

In most cases the parents aren't sufficiently trained in personal finance to really understand their situations. Since the subject intimidates them, it is not surprising that they avoid discussing money matters with their children. Yet the effects of their withholding this information can be devastating.

In my family, Dad's concerns about money made me feel

insecure about the family's finances even though we had everything we needed, including a large house, two cars, etc. Only years later when I was over forty did I find out that all through my childhood my father had budgeted the family expenses a year in advance. In the previous year he had put enough money aside to cover the next year's expenses. If I had known that when I was growing up, I'm sure I would not have been so nervous about not having enough money.

Even in families who are really suffering financial hardship, parents are better off explaining dollars and cents to their kids since they already feel the parents' concern and telling them won't make them feel any worse. In fact, the information will make their plight more real and understandable.

Parents like Ellen's also may not tell their children what their true financial situation is because they may be scared that the children will try to take advantage of the information or inform others about it.

My experience with families who have shared their position is this: When kids know the financial facts, they are much more responsible about living with them and much less likely to talk about them. Moreover, if they are given the responsibility and basic skills for earning and managing their own money, they will have much less fear of it.

Most people who feel strangled by their parents' purse strings don't go to the extreme denial that Ellen did. However, they do develop a poverty mentality, a feeling that they are too poor both spiritually and financially to ever deserve money or have it.

This attitude leads people to deny themselves money as did Ellen or to become obsessed as were her parents. Though I have no evidence to prove it, I would guess that both Ellen's parents also suffered financial abuse when they were growing up, as only people with a deep-seated financial neurosis could deprive their offspring the way they did.

Comparing Ellen's and her parents' ways of handling

anxiety, I'm struck by how they overcompensated in oppo-
site directions. Ellen withdrew, and her parents obsessed.
Yet in each response we see the same basic fear.

Although I wish that I could say Ellen's case is an excep-
tion in family money management, my consulting experience indicates that many people are financially abused by
their families and suffer occasionally.

The sad part is most parents aren't aware that they are
undermining their offsprings' financial identity. They think
they are protecting them when really they are exposing
them to a serious financial illness. In their fear and preoccupation with money they lose perspective on what really
matters in family life.

Yet Ellen proved that people who are suffering from their
families' financial anxieties can overcome them. During the
class I had with her, she was able to remove herself from her
parents' negative attitudes and let go of her feelings of financial deprivation. Though she still resented those
attitudes, she didn't let her feelings interfere with her developing a sound financial plan for herself and her son. When
I last saw her in the school where she was training, she had
just completed six sessions in one day, so I knew she was
motivated to meet her financial goals.

A year later I met Ellen at a school picnic, and she said
she was making it on her own with no support from her
parents. She felt especially proud of herself that she was able
to charge $50 an hour for her services. Yet the scars of her
family history had stayed with her, and she had had to go
into therapy to understand her dysfunctional upbringing.
It took her many sessions to realize that it was her parents
who were dysfunctional and not herself.

It is hoped that our family money histories aren't as de-
structive as Ellen's was, and we can use our own self-awareness to release the fearful money attitudes our parents
drove into us.

PERSONAL EXPERIENCES

In addition to the financial anxieties that germinate in the family, we have to contend with the fears that come from our personal experiences.

As soon as we step out into the world, we are thrown into a melee of financial dealings. By now our egos are trained to upstage our spirits, and we project the financial fears we learned from our families. In such a mental state we often draw to ourselves anxiety-provoking experiences which increase our fearful, negative attitude toward money.

I had such an experience when I was in high school. I felt very uneasy about dealing with money and managing my checkbook. I had managed to survive without mishap as treasurer of my senior class, when, in an unconscious moment, I sent a check used only within the school to pay for my college application. The college returned the check to my dean who sent it back to me with a brief note saying: "Anyone stupid enough to send this check doesn't deserve to go to college."

The news of my carelessness spread fast and soon the class was making a big joke of it. I was mortified, but couldn't stop them from recording it in the yearbook for posterity.

Although eventually I could laugh about it, this early experience left an indelible impression on me. Looking back on it now, I can see it was a natural consequence of my earlier money fears. If I could have dealt with my anxieties then, I'm sure I would have saved myself future embarrassments.

SOCIETY

Ever present is the influence of society which sends out fear-driven messages that money is love, power, happiness, security, and a commodity to be chased after as one's mission in life.

These messages come from social pressures which push us to strive for selfish fulfillment to compensate for the emptiness they feel. Although our spirits may inwardly rebel against these pronouncements, they lack the force required to stifle them.

The disillusionment people have when they subscribe to these beliefs is devastating. They build their lives around getting rich and discover that wealth can't give them the purpose or peace of mind they want.

THE CASE OF THE INNKEEPERS

A good example were innkeepers who asked for my help in planning the sale of their property. This couple, who had two young children, ran a summer inn along the coast. They owned a lovely house adjacent to the inn on a large piece of shore-front property in California. The inn was only breaking even since most of the profits had to be invested in maintaining the place. The family was far from poor, but they weren't rich until the price of shore-front property escalated in value.

Financially it made sense to sell the property since the inn wasn't making money, but the couple at first resisted since they loved the inn and were gifted at running it. However, as land prices continued upward, they got caught up in the profit motive and decided to sell their inn to the highest bidder.

After much negotiation, they took the bid of a developer who razed the inn and built a set of high-priced condominiums. As the couple watched the project going up, they decided they were impelled to live there so they put their house on the market at what they thought was an outrageously high price. It sold very quickly, and they had to move out and rent a place until their condominium was finished.

When they moved into their new residence, they invited

me over to see it. Obviously the husband thought he had won the money game, and a part of him was elated at his victory. But as we sat down for lunch, he turned to me with a baleful look and said, "Now what do I do with my life?"

I couldn't answer him. He had sold himself out of his job, and I knew it would be impossible for him to replace it. He couldn't find a comparable inn to own and didn't want to work for others. He had no other training or job interests. Moreover, running a small inn is a way of life that is hard to duplicate in another job. He loved people and loved serving them on his terms, and the inn gave him that opportunity. Because he also loved where he lived, it would be hard for him to move.

We talked of other possible jobs, but to my knowledge he hasn't found one, and though he lives in comfort, I know he misses having a purpose in life.

The first question we need to ask before we sell ourselves to the highest bidder is the cost to our soul. No amount of money can bribe our soul to be happy, since it works on intangibles such as meaningful purposes, love, and service. If any of these is sacrificed, we suffer.

As painful as striving after the dollar is fighting against it. Many people who don't subscribe to society's money mania spend their lives criticizing it and living in despair over it. I remember a report from a former student of mine that aptly describes this attitude.

PETER'S EVALUATION
OF MONEY AND SOCIETY

"It is clear to me that society judges you by how much money you have. People with a lot of it get special treatment. People without any are thought to be failures.

"When I was twenty, I decided that the only way to change the world was to make tons of money so that I could influence or 'buy' political power. After I started this, I saw that it would take too much money; so I retreated to getting only enough so that I could live unconnected from the 'system.'

"When I discuss political issues, it always boils down to economics of some sort. Usually covert, many times what is hidden behind moralistic or philosophical arguments is, in fact, pure, simple greed."

Peter let his mind get trapped into judging the outward financial inequalities of society and became so overwhelmed by the power structure that he tried to disconnect himself from "the system."

Copping out doesn't get rid of the anxieties. It just makes them linger that much longer. What Peter and all of us need to do is to transform our financially oriented lives into spiritually oriented lives and thereby overcoming our anxieties and perhaps, in a small way, change society's values.

I presented Peter with this challenge, and he was willing to accept it. By the end of the course he had done sufficient work on changing his thinking about money that he could pay his fair share of taxes. For years he had been cheating Uncle Sam by taking excessive deductions. Now he was willing to take only what was due him.

Peter's case ends my brief exploration into the nature of money anxieties. As you can see, we have a challenge before us. Our fears are well embedded and to get them out will take a transformation in consciousness. However, as Ellen and Peter have shown us, it can be done. Even Maria will do it, as you will see in the coming chapters.

Exercises:

1. Take a few moments to reflect on your family's attitude toward money and how it affected you. Write down any negative thoughts, warnings, or rules which may now be influencing you. Examine any negative financial feelings you have from or toward your parents.

2. Review any anxious financial experiences you may have had. See how you created these experiences. Identify any anxieties you may still feel because of them.

3. Evaluate how society influences your attitude toward money. Write a paragraph describing how social institutions like the IRS have affected you.

2

Maria: The Process Begins

"IT SEEMS so overwhelming," were Maria's opening words as she sat down in a chair in my office.

"It really isn't," I replied, as I sat down beside her. "Our first step is to find out where your fears come from. Once we can get at the source of these anxieties we can start to work on them." I paused after saying these words. Then I turned to her and said:

"I want you to take a few moments to think about your father's and mother's attitude toward money."

Maria looked pensive. After a long pause, she answered:

"I can think of only one word that comes to mind when I

consider my family's attitude toward money: obsession."

"That's interesting. Why do you say that?"

"They talked so much about it. Oh! I can remember ump-teen dinner conversations, lectures, and arguments. It was never ending."

"They must have made you feel uncomfortable."

"They did," Maria continued. "Both my parents worried a lot about money. They grew up in the Depression, dirt poor. They made it their life goal to overcome poverty, and they did it." There was no feeling of triumph in Maria's tone.

"So you weren't deprived of money," I said.

"No. I was given everything I wanted," Maria confirmed.

"How did they get their money?" I asked.

"My father joined the marines so that he could go to college. After doing his time, he went to work for a large company and stayed with them for thirty years even though he complained that he was unhappy there. He said he hated his work, but he was very successful and earned enough money to take care of us."

"And your mother?"

"My mother never worked. She stayed at home with us. She didn't go to college. She said they couldn't afford it."

We stopped for a moment. Maria seemed more relaxed. I sensed that sharing this information was doing her some good. I then asked her a question I thought I knew the answer to.

"Did your parents make you guilty about how much they had sacrificed for you?"

"Yes," Maria replied, "all the time." Then she said angrily, "They reminded me so much of how hard they worked for money and for me that I got sick of it!"

We both fell into silence as Maria tried to regain her composure, and I considered her words. It was easy to imagine what Maria had gone through. I had heard many money lectures around our dining-room table. Although I don't think they were meant to make me feel guilty, they usually succeeded in doing so. I tried to console Maria.

"It's difficult when they lay guilt on you. My father did it to me, too. If it's any consolation, I think almost everyone has had a similar experience. I have lots of clients who have the same complaint. I'm sure I did it to my children. Dealing with money is sometimes so frustrating that we feel compelled to take it out on others, especially our family."

"I feel better knowing I'm not alone."

"You certainly aren't. And the sad thing is when parents do this, they also put pressures on us to have the same money priorities as they have. Did your parents want you to make lots of money?" I asked.

"Absolutely. They hounded me on how bad it was to live anything other than a well-off existence. They wanted me to take a high-paying conventional job."

"It's ironic, isn't it? Why should our parents want us to chase after money and suffer the way they did? I've thought about this a lot, and I think their fears of not having enough were so great that they couldn't help thinking that having lots of money was the only way to live."

"I think you're right."

"How did you react to their demands?"

"I rebelled against them. As soon as I got out of college, I joined the Peace Corps."

"To get away from them?"

"Yes, and from worrying about money. I thought the government would take care of my needs."

"I can't blame you. You saw how unhappy they were, and you didn't want to follow in their footsteps."

When I said this, I was reminded of how turned off I had been at the thought of following my father's career in his brokerage business. I had watched him suffer through the pressures of his job and didn't want any part of it or the wealth it could bring.

We paused again. I had another question. "Did they ever try to teach you how to manage your money?"

"No," Maria replied. "They just told me to have 'sound financial management,' without explaining what that meant."

This answer didn't surprise me, and I now felt I knew the basis for Maria's feelings concerning money. Like many people, Maria had been a victim of her parents' financial problems and her own lack of instruction. With no training she couldn't help but be negative and fearful about managing her money since she had only her parents' anxieties and guilt to guide her.

To let go of her parents' attitudes, Maria needed to understand their cause and effect. With this in mind I continued our discussion.

"Maria, I think many of your money anxieties and negativity stem from the guilty feelings your parents gave you."

"I'm sure they did, now that I think about it."

"From what you said, your father was always unhappy because he believed he had to work at a high-paying job he didn't like so that he could support the family in unnecessary luxury."

"That's right."

"And your mother was frustrated with the thought that she couldn't go to college because your father couldn't afford to educate her plus meet your needs."

"Yes."

"All through your life they had reminded you of the financial sacrifice they were making for you, and in living with this smothering guilt you naturally found little comfort in money or your parents' values."

"I see what you mean."

"During those years you also took on many of their money frustrations and fears."

"How did I do that?" Maria asked.

"Unconsciously," I replied. "You acquired their feelings without realizing it. As a child, you were open to their energies and absorbed their fearful attitudes. It was easy for you to do since you had no other belief system to contradict theirs. Although you rebelled against their values, their attitudes stayed with you."

"I never thought of that." There was a glint of real interest in Maria's eyes as she said these words.

"Few people do, but when I suggest it, they usually can recognize common money attitudes between themselves and their parents."

"How do I get rid of these attitudes?" Maria asked.

"I think the best way is to recognize them and forgive your parents for having them. I think your parents did the best they could under the circumstances."

"You do?"

"I think so. They were brought up in poverty and were terrified of returning to it. I believe they didn't know how to stop worrying about their money. It was ingrained in them from their parents and from the actual poverty they endured as children. And it was their need for personal security that prevented them from fulfilling their dreams, not their need to take care of the family as they alleged." Now I had Maria's full attention. I continued.

"They chose to put a priority on making sure they had more than enough money instead of trying to follow their hearts' desires, and they suffered for it. Joseph Campbell tells us that the secret to happiness is to follow our bliss, but their fears were too great to do so. I have nothing but compassion for them."

"I hear what you're saying. It's true they were always afraid about not having enough money. But why did they make me feel bad about it?"

"I think they were simply projecting their frustrations onto you. We all do it. When you think how important money was to them, providing you with it was in their eyes a real act of love. It didn't feel that way to you because it created so many issues."

"You're probably right," Maria consented. "I got so tired

of their arguments I cared less about what they did for me."

"It jaded your whole attitude toward money, and if you don't forgive them and let go of their negative thinking, you'll be stuck with it the rest of your life."

"Why does forgiving them do this?"

"I'm not sure. I just know it works. Forgiving is a means of letting go. It's very effective in getting rid of anger, hate, and other negative emotions."

"I'll have to try," Maria said, sighing.

"One good way is to do a simple visualization exercise."

"How do I do that?" Maria asked.

"You visualize yourself and your parents having a typical money argument. During the argument you express your views in a loving way and ask for their forgiveness. Then you forgive them and yourself and give your parents each a hug."

"Does it really work?"

"It might not work right away, but if you keep doing it and are sincere in your efforts, eventually it will. I think it's effective because it sets up an inner dialogue between you and your parents. You, as you are now, can watch you, as a child, and your parents arguing. You, being removed from the painful feelings, can show compassion to both parties, and the compassion releases the emotions."

"Let's do it."

I took Maria through the visualization (see Exercise 2, p. 23). She chose to relive a particularly painful argument that she and her parents had had concerning her taking a job with the Peace Corps. They had wanted her to get a higher paying job. When the visualization was over, I asked her if it had helped.

"It was hard," Maria responded, "but I was able to hug them." She laughed.

"It will get easier as you work on it. You can use the same visualization to release anxieties you may have gotten from experiences you have had with others."

"By visualizing them instead of my parents."

"Exactly," I replied.

"I can think of plenty of experiences."

"I'm not surprised." I explained to Maria how her current attitude attracted bad experiences, and we agreed she should work on forgiving the people involved in them.

We paused after this discussion as I decided to shift my focus from Maria's parents to her.

"There's another exercise I'd like you to do that can really help you change your attitude."

"What's that?" Maria asked.

"I'd like you to look in the mirror at the beginning of each day and smile at yourself. Try to convey as much love as you can. Then affirm to yourself, 'I *can* manage my money.' Put an emphasis on the *can*. After you do this, take a few moments to review what you are doing that day and what you will need to do with your money."

"You think you can brainwash me into managing," Maria said, laughing.

"Yes," I responded. "You've programmed yourself to be a failure at managing money and you need to change your program. Repeating these words in a loving way every day will give your unconscious the message it needs, and—we hope—inspire you to take care of your daily transactions."

I was reminded of what Edgar Cayce said about mind being the builder. During his lifetime he gave more than 14,000 psychic readings in which he used his mind in trance to effectively diagnose illnesses and prescribe cures for people. I wanted to make sure Maria realized how powerful her mind was.

"You know, Maria, your mind is a powerful tool for changing attitudes. It can do anything you want it to do."

That seemed to convince Maria. "Okay, I'll try it," she said.

"I think we've done enough in this session. What I'd like to do in future sessions is to look at the problems you are having with your finances—cash, checking account, savings, debts, etc., and see if we can't find a more meaningful way of dealing with them—one that's connected to your ideals instead of your fears."

"That sounds good."

* * *

In using Maria as the central example, I'll now take you in the following chapters through a brief exploration of the psychological and spiritual problems of managing personal finances and the philosophy and techniques for dealing with them.

* * *

Exercises:

1. Find a quiet place and take some time to think over how your parents felt about money and how their attitudes affect your attitude. Write a short report describing your thoughts. Keep this report and review it as you work on changing your attitude. This will help you see the progress you are making.

2. A visualization exercise: Sit in a comfortable chair with your back straight. Take a few deep breaths and relax. Close your eyes and clear your mind. Recall a money issue that caused pain between you and your parents. Visualize yourself and your parents standing in a white circle of light reliving that issue. Notice what you are feeling as a child and as an onlooker. Try to feel compassion for your parents. Make sure you express your feelings on the issue. Resolve the issue by having your parents forgive you, and you forgive yourself and your parents. Give each of your parents a hug and let them dissolve out of the circle of light. Open your eyes and slowly come back to consciousness.

3. Do this visualization with anyone else with whom you have had money issues.

4. When you get up in the morning, look in the mirror and smile at yourself. Reflect love onto yourself. Affirm to yourself that you can manage your money. Then review what you are doing that day and what you need to do with your money. Then do it!

3

Practicing Self-Control

Cash

"YOU WON'T tell my husband, will you?" the woman asked with a twinkle in her eye.

"Of course not," I replied, not sure what was coming next. The woman and I had just drawn up a summary of her family's income and expenses, and we couldn't account for $300. I had just asked her if there were any other expenses she had not accounted for.

"Well, every month I slip $100 in cash to each of my three children," she said sheepishly, "and I don't tell my husband because he wouldn't approve."

"That's very kind of you," I said.

"Oh! The kids need it," she responded.

"But I'm not sure you can afford to do this," I replied. "Your summary shows you are overspending by about $200 per month."

"I've had to use my credit card more often since I've been giving this money," the woman admitted.

"Sooner or later your husband will find out from your kids, and he will be upset."

"Yes, I guess you're right," the woman acknowledged reluctantly. "I'll have to cut back on those gifts."

I never heard from this woman again so I don't know if she followed through with what she said. I hoped that after she had stopped giving the money, she would tell her husband what she had been doing. In many cases I find people deceive others and themselves about how they spend their cash, and more frequently than not it gets them into trouble.

I can understand why people want to avoid taking responsibility for what they do with their cash. We all have a history of anxiety-provoking experiences in dealings with it—losses, thefts, disputes, misunderstandings, family criticisms, etc. These experiences often undermine our confidence and make it hard for us to want to manage our cash.

When I ask people if they keep track of their cash, they usually just give me helpless looks. The idea of itemizing their cash expenses is more than they can fathom. Some avoid having cash problems by spending as little cash as possible. However, the majority have a hard time admitting how much cash they actually spend.

To help people manage their cash, I try to get an understanding of their cash habits. When I'm taking down people's financial facts, the first question I ask is how much cash they have in their pockets. Most people are surprised that I'd ask them this as they don't consider their cash an important part of their finances.

I explain that they need to have as complete a picture of

their finances as possible, and cash is a part of it. When people say they aren't sure how much cash they have, I ask them to guess the amount. Then I suggest they count it. Many times I find people's estimates are significantly different from the actual amounts. This simple exercise brings home to them how unaware of their cash they are and helps me assess how hard it will be for them to account for their cash.

One time when I did this with a married couple, it sparked a major issue. The husband had only $5 in his pocket and the wife $56. The husband resented the fact that his wife, who was in charge of their finances, kept most of their money, while he had to borrow from others. Before I could go any further, we had to resolve this issue, and fortunately it was amicably agreed that his wife would allocate him more money.

The husband told me this issue had been smoldering for a long time, but he had been unwilling to talk to his wife about it until I suggested they look at their cash positions. From this case I learned that just revealing people's facts can help them confront their concerns.

After establishing their cash position, I ask people how much cash they use. Almost everyone says that he or she uses very little. However, after we list their expenses in various categories on the summary, I include a separate miscellaneous category for items they've not accounted for—the "leaks," as I call them. These "leaks" range from $20 per month to over $300, with the majority in the $40 to $100 range. Most of these "leaks" are unrecorded cash expenses. For many it's a significant amount of money which tells them they're spending more cash than they think they are.

In motivating them to take better control of their cash, I remind them that their cash spending affects not just their pocketbook but their spirit. When they spend unconsciously, they often buy things that don't bring them real satisfaction.

Most people realize what I'm saying is true when they look at how they spend their cash and see how much they waste on incidental items.

"It's all a matter of practicing self-control," I usually say, and hope they will take that as a goal or ideal to work toward.

As I prepared for Maria's second session, these were some of the ideas that were going through my mind. Before the session I had talked to Maria about how she handled her cash. She said she had given no thought to it. She never kept track of her cash and wasn't conscious of the amounts she spent.

I had asked Maria to write down her cash expenses for the month before our meeting. She had grimaced at this thought, but agreed to do it when I assured her that keeping this record would give her valuable insights about herself and her life style. I guessed from what she told me that she spent much of her cash according to her impulses and moods and that connecting the dollar amounts to these emotions would be the best way for her to find an incentive for redirecting her spending.

She kept her record, and we reviewed it together in our session. As I suspected, she found it quite an eyeopener.

MARIA'S SECOND SESSION

"I never realized I spent so much on junk food," was her initial remark when she saw that she had spent about $50 that month on soft drinks, pastries, potato chips, ice cream, etc.

"It does seem high," I replied. "If you continued to spend at that rate during the year you would spend $50 x 12 months or $600." I paused to let the significance of this calculation sink in.

"I'll have to watch myself," Maria said; and I could tell by the concern in her voice that she understood my point.

I didn't say anything more to Maria about these expenses because I didn't want to seem critical of her habits. In my counseling I find many people spend more than they can afford on sweets and junk foods. For them it becomes a spending addiction. In some cases making people aware of the cost of their habit motivates them to try to control it.

However, many have to recognize the adverse psychological effects this impulse spending has before they are willing to curtail it. Usually when people review their cash expenses and see how much money they've spent on things they didn't need, I'm able to bring to their attention the negative emotional impact of this kind of spending.

We know that spending addictions can't bring us peace of mind, but it takes a lot of inner strength to overcome our emotional need for immediate gratification. I hoped that Maria had this strength.

From Maria's junk-food expenses we moved on to incidental loans and handouts to others. Maria had given out $60, which was more than she could afford. She admitted she was a "soft touch" and rarely got any of her money back.

"I know I can't afford to lend money, so I'm not sure why I do it," she said.

"You may be giving it away out of spite," I said, chuckling. "You said you hated money."

"I know, but that's stupid."

I paused to decide what I should say next. Maria's remark disturbed me. I didn't want her to be overcritical of herself. I was suddenly reminded of what Seth said in Jane Roberts' book, *The Nature of Personal Reality.*[2] Seth said that our beliefs create our reality. While this philosophy doesn't always make sense to me, I could see how Maria's lack of belief in money had led her to give it away. I decided to explain this to Maria. I took a breath and continued.

"You're not stupid, Maria; you're just acting out your belief."

"What do you mean?" she asked.

"I think your beliefs create your reality. So when you have a belief that you hate money, you unconsciously give it away."

"And I'm not even aware of it," Maria said, looking incredulous.

"That's right."

"How can I change this belief?"

"You have to give your unconscious a new belief."

"Like 'I love cash!' " Maria exclaimed, and we both laughed.

"Exactly. However, it's not simply a matter of telling it to your unconscious. You have to inwardly change your present belief."

Maria stopped laughing and considered what I had said.

"You mean get rid of my parents' stuff," she said more seriously.

"Yes. And get in touch with your own feelings."

"But won't I still have my own self-doubts?"

"Yes, you will, but we'll work on them as we go along. I think you'll learn to appreciate your money when you see what it can mean to you." I paused for a moment and then added with a laugh, "And then you won't be so eager to give it away."

"I'd like that," she said and gave me a grin.

We took a short break, and Maria went outside to stretch. When she returned, we resumed our review. Besides junk food and handouts, Maria's expenses didn't seem to concern her, except when she bought a handbag she admitted she didn't need. I asked her to give me the story behind it.

It was on a day she happened to have extra money in her pocket and felt a need to buy something for herself. She had just had an argument with her boyfriend and was feeling depressed. As she was walking along the mall, she spotted the bag. Although she had several, she decided to give herself a present.

"I know it was crazy, but I wanted to feel good about myself," were her words.

"Don't feel guilty," I rejoined. "We're all susceptible to this sort of impulse shopping. But we have to watch out so that our moods don't take us over. They can play havoc with our budget." I laughed as I said this.

"I see what you mean," Maria replied.

"If you can control your mood, you can control your spending."

With these words I ended our discussion of Maria's bag purchase, and we turned once again to her other cash transactions. They included payments for lunches, dinners, movies, gas, and sundry necessities. There were no problems with these expenses so we concluded our session with the understanding that Maria would try to keep track of her junk-food expenses and any money she gave to others.

"I know I can reduce these costs," Maria said as she left my office.

* * *

CHARI

Many people who don't feel as negative about money as Maria still have anxieties managing their cash. A common problem is worrying about being out of control with their spending. In truth their discomfort is with themselves, not with their cash.

I saw this attitude in a middle-aged student named Chari, who spoke to me after attending her first class on money management. She said her main problem was that she used a lot of cash and had no idea where it went. She had no husband, but she had three kids and a house to take care of, and no time to account for her cash.

I guessed that Chari could find the time to record her cash transactions if she were really motivated to do so. However, she probably felt so overwhelmed by the *thought* of having to do it that she rationalized she couldn't.

To enable her to overcome this feeling, I gave her a simple procedure for monitoring her cash, one I knew she had time for.

I suggested she just keep track of the money she kept on hand.

"How do I do that?" she asked.

"Let's start by seeing how much cash is in your pocket," I replied. "Do you know the amount?"

"I think about $100."

"Why don't you count it."

Chari counted her cash and found that she had only $72. She was a little surprised and embarrassed to be so far off.

I assured her that most people didn't know how much is in their pockets. They've never been trained to be aware of this money.

I explained that I had learned from the Buddhists the importance of self-awareness in controlling all aspects of my life, including my pocket money. Just knowing exactly how much we have helps us deal with our anxieties in managing it. When people start keeping track of their cash each day, they automatically review where it has gone, and this acts as a restraint on their impulse spending.

Chari began to monitor her cash, and when I next saw her, she said that she now knew where most of it went. Her largest payouts were to her three children aged ten, twelve, and fifteen. She bought them snacks, gave them generous allowances, and financed their movies, computer games, books, and just about anything they wanted.

Her excuse for doing this was that she had a well-paying job and could afford to be generous.

"But I think it may be out of control," she admitted.

We discussed why she felt such a need to give her kids money.

"I think I feel guilty that I have to be away from them so much," Chari admitted. "I work full time and sometimes in the evening."

"Your guilt is understandable," I said, "but I'm afraid you may be spoiling them."

"It does worry me," Chari lamented.

I paused and thought about Chari's situation. It was not unlike other cases I had had. I have many parents who are single and work full time who tend to spoil their children by giving them too much money. Unfortunately, this doesn't do the children any good as they grow to depend on this money as a substitute for love and then get frustrated and manipulative when they discover it can't satisfy them. I decided I'd have to tell Chari how I felt on this issue.

"Chari, I'll be honest with you. I think you're doing your kids a real disservice by giving them this money. You run the great risk of having them measure your love by how much money you give them, and they will never be satisfied with what they get."

"I know."

"The best thing you can do is to stop giving in to their demands."

"That's going to be hard. I've been doing it for so long, they expect it."

"I know. But I think they'll understand if you explain why you are cutting back, especially if you reinforce what you say by giving them as much individual attention as possible. The more love you can give them, the less demanding they will be."

"I'm sure you're right."

"At first, it may not be easy for them, but I think they are young enough to adjust."

"I'll give it a try."

"I'm sure you can do it. You'll find it easier if you keep as little cash as possible on you. Then when your kids ask for it, you won't have it."

"Good idea."

Another thought occurred to me. "You might also give your children some chores to do for money. It could provide them with the funds they need and teach them a little money management."

"I've just started doing that."

"Good." I felt relieved. I thought Chari understood what she needed to do. It was important she did. I could trace many of my clients' financial problems to their having been given too much money when they were young. They were never taught the value of money and even now couldn't manage it. Many still relied on their families.

We left the subject of Chari's children and moved into another area that gave Chari trouble. Since she always had a lot of cash on her, she was often paying more than her part of the expenses she shared with her friends when they were out together.

"I pretend not to mind, but I really do," was her honest assessment.

"I think we all get irritated when friends take advantage of us," I said, "but it's hard to reject them. You might try carrying less cash on these outings."

Chari looked a little uneasy and admitted she liked having lots of cash with her when she was going out.

I asked her why.

"It makes me feel secure. I don't like using credit cards, and I'm never sure people will take my checks."

"I know what you mean, but the more cash you have, the more likely it is you'll spend it."

"That's true."

"Maybe your fears are exaggerated," I chuckled. "In any case I think you'd have an easier time controlling your generosity if you kept fewer dollars in your purse."

Chari laughed and agreed to try to do with less. Several classes later she recounted the following incident: She was coming back from a movie with her friends when she had a flat tire. The garage man wanted cash for a new tire. Her friends turned to Chari for the money, but she didn't have it so they had to come up with the funds. In discussing the

incident on the way home, Chari was able to tell her friends why she had stopped carrying so much cash.

"They became quite embarrassed," Chari said, "because they knew they had been taking advantage of me. They all apologized, and I felt so much better."

As Chari learned from her experience with her friends, communicating cash concerns to others can lead to more understanding. It can also help us deal with our money hang-ups.

Edgar Cayce put great store in how we handle the little things in life.[3] I find that cash transactions often are little things which can mushroom into traumas if we don't apply the right kind of self-control to our decision making.

*   *   *

Exercises:

1. Count your cash each night and review how you spent it that day. Gradually try to cut back on any impulse spending.

2. Write down your cash transactions in a notebook for a month. Review and evaluate them in light of your priorities. Identify the ones that are done on impulse and try to curb them.

3. Before every cash transaction take a moment to sense if you're really comfortable with it. If you have any doubts, don't do it.

4. Watch your moods as you spend your cash, and see how much they are affecting your spending.

5. If you need to spend less cash, total the amount of cash you take from your paycheck, savings, and other sources during a month. Reduce this amount by 10% and spend only that amount of cash in the following month. Continue to reduce the amount if you need to. Use checks instead of cash when possible.

4

Finding the Right Balance

Checking Account

ALTHOUGH WE know we need to have the right balance in our lives, we rarely think of it when we are managing our checking account! I didn't, until I was faced with the possibility of having thirty-two overdrafts.

It happened when I failed to deposit our monthly paycheck in the right account. By mistake I put it in my own checking account instead of in our joint house account.

I had no idea I'd done this until I received a notice in the mail from the bank that it had refused to accept a check I had written to a charity because of insufficient funds in my account.

The notice came on a Saturday, and I clearly remember how we panicked when we realized its implications. The worst part was that we couldn't do anything about it since the bank was closed.

The notice had taken a week to come to me, and in the interim we had written thirty-one other checks—all of which would bounce if they were returned to my bank during that week. I was mortified at the thought of having to apologize to all the recipients and having to pay the bank $20 an overdraft or $640.

I checked my records, and they indicated that I had deposited the money in the house account, but I also knew that I had deposited money in my own account at the same time, and I couldn't be sure the paycheck had gone into the right account.

Leila and I reviewed our plight and realized that we had to see a bank officer when the bank opened on Monday morning to stop any further overdrafts. If it had been the teller's fault, we would ask the bank to make amends.

We went in Monday morning and discovered that although the bank had refused to pay the charity check, it had paid seventeen other checks that had come in. The bank officer, named Mary, didn't know why it had paid the others.

We tallied up the cost of the eighteen overdrafts and they added up to $360. Mary said she would discuss this cost with us when we found out who was responsible for the error.

The next day Mary called and said that I had used the wrong deposit slip, and since it was my error would I agree to pay $180, half of the overcharge fees. I said we didn't think that was fair since we believed the bank was wrong in not calling us about the overdraft as soon as it came in. Mary said that she would review it again.

She called back that day and told us that the bank would not charge us for any overdraft. She said that these things happen, and she realized that the bank had caused us a lot of stress.

I felt humbled and appreciative of the humanness the people at the bank had shown. They had not only paid my overdrafts and absorbed the penalties, but forgiven me for my error.

Before this incident I hadn't given much thought to the spiritual implications of managing my checking account, but after struggling through this experience, I realized how much of an emotional impact it could have.

In my consulting I find the checking account to be a source of many money anxieties—so much so that some people can't bring themselves to keep any checkbook records. Whereas they love spending money, they hate keeping track of it. Consequently, they often live with the fear of not knowing how much is in the account.

After many years of helping people deal with these accounts, I'm convinced that confronting our checkbooks is just another way of confronting ourselves. We need to look at our balances with as much care as we look at our health since they both affect how we feel.

Many of us live on an emotional roller coaster with our money. When there is plenty in the bank, we feel up; when there is little, we feel down. These swings create stress, and to avoid them we need to learn to control our feelings and our balances.

These were some of the thoughts I wanted to share with Maria in our third session.

* * *

MARIA'S THIRD SESSION

In preparation for our session I asked Maria how she handled her checking account. She said she wrote checks when she needed to, but had trouble remembering to fill in her stubs. She just laughed when I asked her if she balanced her account. I told her it would be good if she got an accurate balance from her bank for our session.

When we met, Maria had gotten her balance and found that she had only $10 left in her account. She was upset, as she had just written two checks for a total of $52 which was not covered by her balance. She was depositing her paycheck this week in the hope that it would be there in time to cover her checks.

"It's pretty unnerving when we have to deposit money to cover our checks," I said sympathetically.

"Yes it is," she replied. "I know it's my own fault. If I paid attention, this wouldn't happen. I hope I won't get an overdraft."

"You won't be alone if you do," I replied. "If it's any consolation, I think most of the population gets overdrafts." I laughed. "Even sophisticated business people make errors in their personal checkbooks. I've seen them."

Hearing these words, Maria began to relax. She sat back in her chair and looked at me curiously.

"Why do they make them?" she asked.

"I'm not sure," I replied. "I think part of it is that they're nervous about their money. A doctor once said to me he played 'peekaboo' with his checkbook. He'd write checks without looking at his balance because he was afraid to see how much money he was spending." We both laughed as I said this, and I felt Maria's anxieties recede. I continued.

"I think the doctor expresses a good reason for possible errors—money anxieties. I know when I'm working on my account and I'm worried about my money, my mind has a tendency to wander, and I can easily make a wrong calculation."

"I can identify with that doctor's feelings," Maria exclaimed, "and I don't even *look* at my bank statement!"

"I think many people don't," I replied, "and it might not be necessary if we kept good accounts and the bank never made errors. But everyone makes mistakes, even the bank."

"I wouldn't know," Maria said, and I could tell she was trying to make a joke.

I smiled and continued, "I usually try to balance my checkbook every month. Yet I remember one time I didn't, and the bank made a $300 error against me. It was during the fall, and we were so busy that it was three months before I found time to do my balancing. I had three statements to reconcile. I went through the statements and found the $300 difference, but couldn't find the error. Finally I asked Leila to look for it, and she discovered it. The bank had erroneously charged me $300, but it didn't show up as a special charge. They had made a wrong entry on an insurance payment and I had missed the error. If I hadn't attempted to balance the account, we would never have caught the error."

"That's a big mistake," Maria said, and her eyes widened. She shook her head. "I know I should balance my account, but it's hard to bring myself to do it."

I paused to think about what to say next. I knew what Maria was talking about. Many shared her lack of will power not only for balancing but for keeping track of their account. In dealing with this problem with others, I'd had success when I talked about the need to avoid the stresses that went along with managing this money. Thinking Maria might be persuaded by this approach, I had even brought a list of these stresses from a book I'd recently read. I decided now was the moment to broach the subject.

"Maria, it might help if you think of managing your checking account as just another way of bringing balance into your life." I paused to make sure she was with me.

"I think balancing our checking account is just as important as balancing our diet, work, and play, since it has the same potential for creating stress."

"I never thought of it causing me stress," Maria said.

"I had it brought home to me when I was reading an essay by Hans Selye,[4] and he had a list of self-perceived symptoms of stresses. Many of them I could easily identify with when I'm worrying about my money. They made such an impression on me that I jotted them down. I have them here."

I showed Maria the list.

Symptoms of Stress

1. General irritability
2. Pounding of the heart
3. Dryness of the mouth
4. Impulsive behavior
5. The overpowering urge to cry or to run and hide
6. Inability to concentrate, flight of thoughts, and general disorientation
7. Feelings of unreality
8. "Floating anxiety"—that is, being afraid yet not knowing what you're afraid of
9. Insomnia
10. Excess sweating

"I can identify with all of them," Maria said with a laugh, "especially the one about having the urge to run away."

"I like the 'floating anxiety' one best," I rejoined, "since it so aptly describes how I feel when I don't know how much money is in my account. I think it's the 'not knowing' that causes much of my insecurity."

"Except if I know I don't have any money," Maria quipped.

"Yes, of course. But just think, if we can reduce any of these symptoms by simply taking care of our checking account, wouldn't it be worth the effort?"

"You do have a point," Maria answered.

"And the effort doesn't have to be that great," I paused. Now that I had Maria's attention, I was going to give her the easiest way to manage a checking account.

"If you would just look at the balance in your checkbook every day, you would reduce your stress," I said.

"How's that work?" she asked.

"Simple. By monitoring your balance daily, you get to know how much is in your account. Just knowing the amount will relieve you of most of your anxiety." I looked at Maria to see if she agreed. She nodded.

I continued, "As you look at your balance, you'll see when you have forgotten to put your check information on your stub, and you'll be reminded to do it. Since the transaction will be fresh in your mind, you'll have no trouble recalling it."

"I get it," Maria exclaimed with a laugh. "You're going to make me keep better records!"

"Right," I replied with a smile, "and you'll feel much less stress because you'll know where you stand with the account." I paused to see if Maria was convinced. She seemed to be.

"That doesn't sound too difficult," she acknowledged.

"It isn't, and the feedback I get from my clients is that it really works."

"What about balancing my checking account. Do I still have to do that?" Maria asked.

"I would. The way I handle my bank statement is this: As soon as it comes in, I compare it to the balance in my checkbook. I know the amounts will be different since there will be bank charges and checks outstanding, but I can at least tell if I have a major discrepancy which requires immediate action. If I do, I balance the account right away. If not, I may wait a week or more before reconciling the account."

"That sounds like a good way of doing it," Maria said.

"It works for me," I said.

We were both silent. It was time our meeting ended. I started to get up when Maria announced, "I think I'll start by looking at my balances."

"Fine," I said, and then I had one other thought. "It might

help also if, before writing out a check, you took a moment to reflect on the transaction. If you have any doubts, you can always hold off on it."

"That's a good idea."

"Try it; I think it will save you money."

On these words our session came to a close.

* * *

JEREMY

I neglected to tell Maria that just reviewing her check payments could be another effective way to overcome stress and save money. I had a case of a hospital manager named Jeremy who didn't believe he could control his money. He had three children in college and a lot of expenses. He said he had tried drawing up a budget once, but it hadn't helped.

"I've never tried again," he said. And I could tell from his tone that he felt the task was hopeless. "So far I've gotten along okay, but I still worry a lot about my money."

"At least you're willing to admit it. Most people aren't that honest with themselves."

We sat in silence for several moments, as I considered what to say next.

"How many accounts do you have?" I asked.

"I have one, and my wife and I have a joint account, and she has one. That's three," he answered.

"I think that's a good way to manage money when you have spouses or partners. You can work all your karma[5] out through the joint account," I said laughingly.

"You're right," he chuckled.

"Seriously," I said, "I do recommend to couples who are just starting out to use a joint account in order to share their joint expenses. It may cost a little more, but it forces them to work together with their money."

"It works well for us."

"Good. I also suggest that couples put money into it on a proportional basis, according to how much they can afford, and then treat the money as if it were for either of them. I tell them it's an experiment in learning 'oneness.' " I smiled at Jeremy and he smiled back. We paused for a moment. Then I asked him:

"Do you balance your joint account?"

"No, my wife does," he replied.

"You might find it useful to do it yourself for a while. It will help you understand where your money is going."

Jeremy didn't say anything, but I could see he didn't really believe me. He still had his budget experience fresh in his mind.

"I've been letting her take care of that. I'm so busy," he replied.

"But if you want to work on getting rid of your fears, confronting your checkbook is the best place to start," I persisted.

"Is it?" he asked skeptically.

"Well, it's from there that most of your money is spent. There are so many hidden costs that we don't see until we write the checks for them. It's easy to feel overwhelmed when we don't know where our money is going."

"It makes sense," he said reluctantly.

"And if you take the time to go over your joint check payments, you'll probably find some ways to save money," I said.

"I'll give it a try, and tell you what I find," he said.

And we left it at that.

I wasn't sure I'd hear from Jeremy since he didn't seem convinced by what I had said. But several months later, I received a call from him. To my surprise he said he had been balancing their joint account and reviewing their check payments and had to admit he found it less stressful knowing how "his money vanished," as he put it. He also stated that he felt more in control of his life now that he was more conscious of their spending.

He did find that he was paying over $50,000 for his kids'

tuitions and wondered if there was some way he could stretch out his payments. He had been sending them checks for the total amount in August.

I suggested he negotiate with the colleges to pay them twice a year—perhaps August and February. This would permit him to earn interest on the money he was holding back. We ended this conversation with Jeremy agreeing to contact the colleges.

Several weeks later Jeremy called again. He had talked to the colleges and was able to change the payments. He estimated he would earn more than $500 in interest on the money he had been able to keep. We ended this conversation agreeing that reviewing check payments did indeed provide constructive benefits!

*   *   *

Jeremy recognized a very important function that managing a checking account can provide—that of helping us control ourselves. Often when people come to me whose lives and spending are out of control, I use their checking account to help them control their costs. First, I have them draw up their monthly income and expenses. From these figures we estimate how much money they need to live on each month. Then I suggest they take that money from their job income or other sources, put it in their checking account, and live off of it. They can use credit cards, but only if they pay the total balance each month.

Those who try this approach tell me it immediately brings results. Being forced to stay within their checking account funds also forces them to live within their means. In the process they learn how to plan, since in order to make the money last through the month, they have to portion it out.

GEORGE AND JOANNA

I used a similar approach with George and Joanna, a recently retired couple from Texas, who came to me because they were having trouble financing Joanna's hobby, traveling. In their case, however, there was much more involved than simply getting control of their spending.

While George was working, there had always been plenty of money for Joanna's trips. But when he retired and decided to go back to school, he was afraid his retirement income wouldn't cover his education costs and her travels.

When he tried to discuss his fears with Joanna, she responded with her own agenda of concerns. She resented the fact that she had always had to manage the household business—checkbooks, bills, etc. She had spent her life taking care of these things. Now that the children were away from home and he was retired, she wanted him to take more responsibility. When he signed up for the courses, she saw it as a way for him to once again relegate the work to her.

Their problems were made more complicated by their lack of communication. George took care of the investments, Joanna the daily bills. They did their tasks very separately. Each kept his and her own checking account and rarely talked to each other about what they were doing. Since George had earned most of the money, he controlled what they lived on and parceled it out to Joanna. This had been okay with Joanna as long as he was working, and they had more than enough money. Now that he was retired and they had less income to live on, Joanna wanted to have an equal say in how it was managed.

When I heard George and Joanna's story, I realized they were dealing with the common issues of power and responsibility that so often undermine couple relationships. As in so many cases, their money concerns were only symptoms of these deeper issues.

I started our session by asking George to explain the

sources of their income. He made a list of the income they received from their investments and retirement money. Then I had Joanna outline their monthly expenses. Just sharing these facts brought the couple closer together as each got to understand the other's side of the financial picture. After reviewing their income and expenses, they found that they didn't have enough income to pay for two trips that Joanna had planned plus pay for George's education costs.

Joanna felt she deserved the trips and thought that they should use his capital to pay for them. George was reluctant to do this as he was afraid they'd run out of money.

To break their impasse I suggested that they look at the investments to see if they could make any changes which might increase their income. George had invested his money mostly in common stock funds which paid an income of only 3% dividends. I suggested that they liquidate half of their stock funds and put the proceeds in bond funds that were currently paying 7% interest. The switch would increase their income by $5,000. George liked this plan since he would be getting more money and wouldn't have to take any out of capital. And it satisfied Joanna because it provided the income they needed for their separate projects.

Once they agreed to this investment change, much of the tension between them dissolved. However, Joanna still thought it was unfair that she had to be totally responsible for managing their daily affairs.

I suggested that they set up a joint checking account and share the maintenance of it. I said it would be a good way for them to work out their money differences. I also advised them to put a fixed amount into the account each month based on their monthly expenses and live within that income, paying off their credit cards each month. Doing this would give them a simple means of budgeting their costs.

They accepted these ideas, and when I next saw them George was monitoring their expenses as well as managing the joint account and taking courses, while Joanna was flying off to Kenya.

*   *   *

As we can see from these cases, money concerns are directly related to our human frailty. In my case, the overdrafts were a result of my carelessness; in Maria's, the impulse spending was a consequence of low self-esteem; in Jeremy's, his lack of control came from a false belief that he couldn't manage his money; and in George and Joanna's, their budgeting problems were caused by their failure to communicate and share responsibility. In each case changing the approach to managing the checkbook played a vital part in solving these problems.

Chinese medicine says that balancing energies is essential to finding health and wholeness. Similarly, balancing the money flowing in and out of our checking account is a basic antidote to the stress of managing it.

Exercises:

1. Look at the balance in your account(s) each day, and keep your check stubs up-to-date.

2. Look at your bank statement as soon as it comes in and compare the bank's balance figure with the balance in your checkbook. If the difference suggests a possible problem, balance your account immediately. If not, balance it as soon as convenient.

3. Review your check payments each month. Make sure you are spending money according to your priorities. Look for ways to save money.

4. Before signing any check take a few moments to see if the payment feels right. If you have any doubts, hold off on the transaction.

5

Preserving Yourself

Savings and Investments

SAVINGS AND investments are more meaningful when we think of them as a reserve energy which can not only help preserve ourselves but also give us what we need to develop our full potential. The act of saving is an act of self-love. It says we are worth being taken care of.

In consulting I discovered that those who know how to save are far more centered and at peace with themselves than those who can't. This makes sense since to save requires discipline and self-control—two necessities for having inner calm.

Many of us tend to think we are worth less as individuals

if we have less money, and merely telling ourselves how valuable we are doesn't change our attitude. We need to *feel* it. Saving money can be a powerful way of giving ourselves that inner confirmation.

As children, we were never brought up to think of savings as a source of personal growth. Many of us first learned about savings when we were given a piggy bank for saving our coins. We were instructed that if we wanted to buy something we couldn't afford, we should save up for it. With that brief explanation we were harnessed with a belief that savings was only important for what it could buy in the future. Many of us tried to save for a while, but sadly the habit didn't "take" and, after saving up for several "wishes," we gave up.

There were some, however, who were exceptions; such as a nine-year-old brother of a student of mine who saved not only money but everything, including the candy he got on Halloween. My student said that her brother would weigh the candy after it came in, put it in the bottom drawer, and eat it slowly so that it would last until Easter! Oh, if only we could handle our dollars in the same careful way!

In young adulthood we needed all the money we could get just to take care of our bursting needs and wants. The dollars we earned from our summer and part-time jobs went to our education and/or our survival, and any funds that went into savings accounts were usually only there for very brief spans of time. During this period our money gyrated up and down just as our moods did and never settled in our pockets for very long.

Here is a report from a student, named Wendy, which aptly describes the financial turmoil of those years:

WENDY'S REPORT

"At the age of eighteen, after having little or no training in the art of money management, I was willingly cast into the world. I moved in with my sister where I promptly found a job . . . I was not always frugal, nor always extravagant, but seemed to swing from one extreme to another. Mostly I kept my bills paid and never used credit. Some days I had a great deal of money and others (more often) I had hardly any money at all . . . At that time nothing was saved for more than a few weeks."

Wendy's topsy-turvy spending and lack of savings are very understandable when we see them in the context of the emotional instability that characterized her adolescence. Fortunately as she grew older, her emotions settled down, and she was able to plan her finances more carefully and save some money.

However, others aren't able to let go of their adolescent money insecurities and fall into the fallacy of believing that they never can save money.

This was the state of mind that Maria was in when we discussed savings and investments in our fourth session.

Maria had no savings or investments.

MARIA'S FOURTH SESSION

"I've never been able to save a dime," was her opening remark.

"Why not?" I asked.

"Oh! I don't know. I just can't do it," she said, shaking her head.

"I know you can," I replied. "It's just that you haven't thought it was worth it. You may have a mental block against savings just the way you do about your money."

"You mean my family prevented me from wanting to save."

"That's partly it. They made dealing with money such a burden that you had little incentive to save it."

"I see."

"But it may also be tied in with your own self-image. You may never have felt good enough about yourself to want to save for yourself."

Maria seemed surprised by this idea, but didn't reject it. After a pause she said, "I like the idea of having some extra money, but I make so little it doesn't seem real to try to save it."

"Why not? All it takes is a little discipline. You don't have to save much. Just a few dollars each week."

"Where would I put it?" she asked.

"In a cookie jar," I said with a laugh. "Any place will do. Seriously, when you go to your bank to deposit your paycheck in your checking account, you can take some money out and put it in a savings account."

"It wouldn't be very much."

"That doesn't matter. For you the act of saving is a confirmation of your own self-worth."

"I never thought of it that way," she said, smiling, and I knew she understood what I was saying.

We sat in silence for a moment. Then a puzzled look came over her face.

"What if I need the money?" she questioned.

"You can take it out if you want. It would be better if you could forget about it and pretend you didn't have it, at least until you've built up a good reserve. But if you take some out, be sure to continue to save every week."

"Okay, I'll try."

"Good. I think that's all we'll cover today. I don't want to overwhelm you with investment information until you've saved enough to make it worth investing. For now, just remember, it's the act of saving that's important."

*　*　*

Assuming Maria is able to save money, she will eventually be faced with the daunting task of knowing how to invest it. I started her off with the savings account because that was the easiest and most appropriate vehicle to use. But as she accumulates money, she will have to look at other alternatives.

MARK

One faced with this dilemma was a young trainee named Mark who came to see me. He had $400 of uncashed checks in his hand. Mark had just started a six-month training program for a large company. Since most of his living costs were covered by the company, he had saved this extra money and wanted my advice on what to do with it.

He said that he was almost persuaded to buy life insurance from one of his co-workers who guaranteed him 8% interest on the savings plan that went along with it. I asked him if he had any need for life insurance. Mark said he didn't. He had no family to leave money to. I explained the cost of buying the insurance and the limitations of his getting the money out, and he realized the investment wasn't appropriate.

Mark then said he'd like to go into the stock market. He'd been watching it during the last several months and it had been going steadily up. He thought if he bought a common stock and sold it while the price was going higher, he could make some quick money.

I explained that there was a risk in buying stocks since the stock market fluctuated a lot, and it was impossible to anticipate when it might go down. If he were willing to hold on to the stock for several years, he'd have a much better chance of making money than if he tried to buy and sell quickly. In Mark's situation I couldn't recommend his buying stocks since trading them would be too risky.

Mark was disappointed when I suggested he put the funds in a regular savings account since it paid only 5% interest. But I told him he might need the money to cover his living costs once his six-month training plan was over, and the savings account was the best way to save his funds and be sure of having them available for this kind of contingency.

Reluctantly, Mark took my advice; later I heard from his parents that he was glad he had. He had gotten into an argument with his boss and left the company and was using his savings to live on while he found another job.

* * *

Following the piggy bank logic which we were brought up with usually leads us to adopt a simplistic "greed" approach to investing that Mark was considering. This approach focuses on our making as much money as possible on our investments.

This approach is fraught with peril because it doesn't take into account the individual's practical and spiritual needs. Looking at investments as personal energy helps us see their real connection to us. Every investment should help us gain peace of mind as it contributes to our sense of security. Mark had to forego investing in illiquid or risky investments in order to have the contentment of knowing that his funds were accessible and safe. If he hadn't had to meet this criterion, he could have put his money in more aggressive investments.

When I worked as a stockbroker, I saw many men and women get caught up in trying to make money in the stock market. Unfortunately it was during the time of the oil crisis when the stock market was going down. As the value of their investments declined, many became disillusioned with the market and themselves. The ones who survived the sell-off the best were those who believed in their stocks and were willing to hold them until stock prices went back up. The nonbelievers usually sold their stocks when the prices were down and lost money on them.

The believers weren't afraid of holding on to their stocks because they had faith in their companies. They had invested according to what they believed and, as a consequence, suffered no guilt or remorse when their stock lost value.

Until I went through that long market decline, I never thought of applying my spiritual beliefs to buying stocks; but when I saw how well the believers handled that difficult time, I decided it was an essential part of the investment process.

We owe it to ourselves to choose those investments that we can believe in. But we also must be sure they are appropriate to our circumstances and that they have sufficient economic potential to make them a good investment.

ALEX

There are times when we have no choice but to accept investments that we don't believe in. I had a case in which I had to advise a client named Alex to hold on to Coca Cola® stock even though I knew he didn't like the products. His father had purchased the stock at an adjusted cost price of 75¢ a share before he gave it to him. If the son sold the stock, he would have had to pay 33% of the proceeds in capital gains taxes because he had to assume his father's low cost price.

Over the years Coca Cola had done very well, and Alex had made a lot of money on the stock despite his disillusionment with it. Many analysts thought the company would do well in the future. I felt obliged to tell Alex that he should hold the stock and borrow against it if he needed money. By taking a loan on the stock, he could get money from it without having to sell it.

In presenting this alternative, I told Alex he might find it meaningful to think of the stock symbolically in terms of his relationship to his father. Alex had had a lot of trouble accepting his father, just as he had had difficulty accepting his father's Coca Cola stock. Perhaps in having to accept the stock, Alex was being reminded that he had to accept his father.

Often I have people come to me with wonderful "spiritual" investments which have no financial backing. I have to remind them that for an investment to be successful, it must live up to financial standards as well as spiritual ones.

No matter how much we believe in our investments, we shouldn't be attached to them. The Buddhists have the right idea when they say we should practice detachment in our material life. We shouldn't let our egos get caught up in the successes or failures of investments because then investing becomes an emotional trauma, and we lose a major part of the benefit of it. Even though an investment makes us rich, if it creates debilitating stress and anxiety, it isn't worth owning. Our soul is more important than our net worth.

On the other side, we have to be willing to accept our losses with our gains, since they are an essential part of investing. As with any of life's endeavors, there is always a negative with a positive.

HELEN

Accepting losses isn't easy to do, as a client named Helen found out. She came to me for advice about selling the silver she owned. A year before, Helen had purchased 6,250 ounces at $5 an ounce. Her total cost was $31,250. When she appeared on my doorstep, the current price of silver was $40 per ounce and her holdings were worth $250,000. She had made over $200,000 in a year.

When I saw the size of the profit, I said I'd be tempted to sell at least part of the position to protect her profit. However, Helen had just received a report from an investment firm assuring her the price had to go higher.

We looked at all the economic data, and everything

pointed to the investment firm's prognosis—a doom and gloom scenario for everything but the price of gold and silver. Helen was enthralled by this scenario and decided to keep her position.

A month later the price of silver started to drop. I spoke with Helen about selling some of her silver, but she was determined to hold on. She was so sure she was right.

Within two years the price of silver went down to $4 per ounce, and Helen, instead of having over $200,000 of profit, had a $6,250 loss.

When I talked with her about what had happened, she was naturally crestfallen not to have sold her silver sooner. She realized she had made her investment into a symbol of her economic beliefs that she couldn't give up. In this case she wasn't too attached to the silver, but to her own beliefs.

Helen had learned her lesson, however, and had the courage to humbly accept her losses. With that acceptance also came self-forgiveness, and to my knowledge she has never suffered further remorse or guilt.

As Helen found out, investing is a spiritual challenge, and the yardstick for measuring it is our feelings toward it as well as its potential pay out.

In another case that also involved the loss of profits in the stock market, a client named Anne learned what her losses were really worth.

ANNE

Anne came to me because she was frustrated with her financial advisor. She was dissatisfied with her investments, but couldn't get her advisor to make any changes.

She was a peace activist and didn't want to support any companies associated with war or polluting the air. Her portfolio included stocks representing car, chemical, and defense companies, and she wanted them exchanged for more socially conscious investments.

When Anne complained about her investments, the advisor wouldn't listen to her, as he believed that they were good money makers and that was all that was important. He felt he was the expert, and she should follow his advice.

Anne showed me her investments, and I could see why the advisor didn't want to sell them. They represented "blue chip" (i.e., the best) companies that her family had given her. They were safe and sound and their cost was very low. If they were sold, she would have to pay a large capital gains tax.

I explained this to Anne, and she understood the advisor's position, but still wanted to get rid of the stocks. Moreover, she didn't like the patronizing way the advisor dealt with her. He was constantly putting her down and making her feel helpless.

I asked Anne how long she had been working with this advisor, and she said about five years. Her father had been working with him on the family's investments for many years, and at his request she had kept him on after her father could no longer manage the funds.

I suggested that the advisor might represent more than an investment guide. He could symbolize her father's control over her. Anne agreed that this was the case and that indeed she needed to let go of him for her own peace of mind. We looked at the possibilities of her having other advisors, but none seemed to fit, so she decided to manage her investments herself, with my help.

We reviewed her portfolio and decided that since she didn't need to make money in the stock market and was afraid of investing in it, she should sell all her stocks and put her funds in a socially conscious money market fund.

Unfortunately, after she sold her stocks, the market soared, and many of the stocks she had owned doubled in value.

I had been watching the stock market and was aware that our timing had been bad, so I wasn't surprised when she came to my office full of concern. However, her opening words really startled me.

"You know, this is my father talking," is what she said, and that was just how I would have expected her father to sound. For a moment I actually thought I was talking to her father!

Her tone was restrained, but I felt her frustration as she judged me and herself for selling her stocks. I could see her regress to her father's dollars-and-cents mode, and I was concerned that she might not be able to come out of it.

Suddenly I found myself asking her how she felt about not owning any stocks.

Immediately her face relaxed into a smile as she confessed that it was such a relief not to have to think about her stocks or listen to Louis Rukeyser's investment commentaries on *Wall Street Week!*

This realization immediately brought her out of her father's energy and into her real self. I asked her if the basis of her anxieties and frustration might be not that she had lost an opportunity to make money, but rather that she didn't fulfill her father's management goals.

She nodded her head in agreement, and we both had a good laugh at the Jekyll and Hyde performance. As soon as she understood that it was her father's anxieties she was manifesting and not her own, her worries about selling the stocks disappeared.

I asked her about her father's attitude toward money and how it may have influenced her. She said he came from a very conservative background that instilled in her an exaggerated importance of hanging on to money and managing it well. Since her mother had no influence or interest in finance, her father laid down the financial laws.

Money was not discussed in the family, and Anne was never taught or encouraged to manage her own investments. Right into her middle age Anne's inheritance was managed by her father until he was too old to do so. He had lived through the Depression and had a great fear of losing money. To him "blue chip" stocks were a sure bet and shouldn't be sold.

Thus when Anne rebelled against her father's dictates by selling her stock, she felt guilty for having gone against her father's wishes—an emotional throwback to her family past.

By talking through these issues, she was able to free herself from her father's bondage and accept the financial responsibility for her life. Our session ended with the understanding that the money lost by getting out of the stock market was not as significant as the independence gained from breaking out of an old financial pattern.

Though our psychological attachments can be a real impediment to managing investments, the biggest roadblock is our genuine fear of doing it. To overcome this anxiety, I make a list of the types of investments and explain to people how each of them works. I suggest, if they've never invested before, that they start by purchasing safe investments until they are confident enough in their investment ability to buy more aggressive ones. For those who already have investments I have them look at the cost, current value, and annual income of each investment. Just looking at these facts inspires people to manage because they immediately see changes they can make to improve their position.

MARTHA

Martha was a good example. She came to me with a portfolio of bonds and stocks that she knew nothing about. She had gotten them from her husband's estate, and he had managed them himself until he died. She had no experience in investing and was afraid of making any changes.

I explained to her how each investment worked and had her write down its cost, current value, annual income, and annual return (the annual income divided by the current value).

When she looked at her total return on her investments and found that she was getting only 4%, she was eager to change them for higher paying ones.

We then reviewed the facts on each investment and what each produced, and she could see by comparing the cost and current value and the income returns which ones were making her the most money and which produced the kind of products and services she approved of. We kept these in- vestments and sold the rest.

I then explained how mutual funds worked, and she re- alized that by comparing their investment performances she could choose the best ones without fear of making a mistake. She knew her money would be well invested be- cause of their excellent long-term performance. With the help of a stockbroker she selected several funds which over the next year would increase her income by $4,000. From then on she was no longer fearful of running her invest- ments!

The trick to anxiety-free investing is in knowing the ap- propriate choices. With this knowledge you can detach yourself from its ups and downs.

But, as I said to Martha, whether you learn to invest or not isn't as important as learning how to save. In money management that's the most important means of attaining peace of mind.

* * *

Exercises:

1. Begin to save. Take money and put it aside as an act of self-love. Whenever you receive a paycheck, take a portion of it and put it in a savings account.

2. When you want to purchase an investment, make a list of your alternatives. Find out how they work and what they produce. At first choose a safe investment that you *believe* in. When you have confidence in your investing ability, consider a more aggressive investment. Be sure to understand its potential risks and rewards, and remember that it needs to fit in with your spiritual ideals and goals as well as your need to make money.

4. If you already own investments, do an evaluation of them by examining what they do and comparing their cost, current value, annual income, and return. (Divide its annual income by its current value to calculate the percentage of return. For example, if a common stock's current value is $5,000 and it pays $100 in dividends, its return is 2%—$100 divided by $5,000.)

5. Before making an investment, take a few moments to make sure the investment feels right. If you have any doubts, hold off on the purchase.

6

Valuing Yourself

Job Income

IT NEVER occurred to me to think of my pay as spiritual recompense when I began my career as a stockbroker. I had been inculcated in my growing-up years with the idea that job income was security and an important measure of my value as a human being.

Under this delusion at the tender age of twenty-five, I began selling stocks. I had prepared myself well and soon had a growing business specializing in managing small company pension and profit-sharing funds which were trusteed by banks. When my brokerage house asked me not to solicit any more of this business, I decided to move to another firm.

A friend asked me to join his firm's investment department. I had an interview with the department head, and he
promised me a big pay increase with all sorts of benefits. I
was so impressed with his promises that I didn't think
through all the ramifications—not the least of which being
the character of my boss.

After six months of working in his department, I realized
my boss was overly threatened by my work. I didn't know
how much until one day I was called into a senior partner's
office and told, to my dismay, that my boss had recommended that I seek psychiatric help. He thought that he felt
I was unbalanced. Since my boss was the senior partner's
nephew, I felt I had no recourse but to see the psychiatrist
the partner suggested.

The next day during work I wrote a short letter to one of
my customers. My boss reviewed the letter and changed almost every word in it. The corrections were so absurd that I
took the letter to the psychiatrist. He reviewed the letter and,
without saying a word, picked up the phone, called the senior partner, and gave me a clean bill of health. As I went
out of the psychiatrist's office, I thanked the Universe for
giving me that letter!

This experience forced me to ask myself what my job really meant to me. Believing that a job was just a way to make
a lot of money didn't make sense, as no amount was worth
the suffering I went through during those six months.

In searching for an answer, I came across a passage in the
Bhagavad Gita, the ancient spiritual epic from India, which
spoke to me. In this passage Krishna says:

"This man of harmony surrenders the reward of his work
and thus attains final peace: the man of disharmony, urged
by desire, is attached to his reward and remains in bondage."[6]

This passage reinforced what I knew in my heart but had
not been willing to acknowledge: that my job had to be fulfilling to my spirit. In chasing after money I had separated

my job objectives from my spiritual objectives, thus becoming "the man of disharmony" who "is attached to his reward and remains in bondage." My pay had to be seen as a spiritual recompense as well as a material one.

Mercifully while I was doing this reevaluating, I was allowed to leave the investment department and join the ranks of the independent stockbrokers. I stayed in this job for several more years until I felt it could no longer satisfy me. Then I left it for a simpler life of consulting and writing.

The memory of that experience in the investment department and Krishna's words stayed with me, and when I was asked to help evaluate people's salaries and job benefits, I made it a point to examine their spiritual value as well as their dollar value.

These examinations were never easy. People weren't comfortable discussing their pay. They were afraid that I would judge them on how much they made. Many thought they weren't paid enough, yet they didn't have the courage to discuss the matter with their superior. Most knew how much they grossed and netted, but few kept track of their deductions. The majority tended to evaluate their job mostly on how much they were making and had difficulty measuring it by spiritual standards.

To help people with their job income problems, I always look at their practical concerns in the context of their spiritual dilemmas, as you will see in Maria's case.

Maria had told me that she had given little thought to her income when she was working for the Peace Corps and had spent the money she had saved abroad when she returned to the U.S. Right after leaving the Peace Corps, she had applied to take courses in social work. She didn't have the money, but she hoped to earn it.

Before this session I told Maria that as part of the "Money and Spirit" course she was taking with me, she would have to come up with a job plan for supporting herself, and since she hadn't done it before and had expressed anxiety about doing it, I thought it would be helpful if we used this session to discuss it.

MARIA'S FIFTH SESSION

"How are you supporting yourself now?" was my initial question as we started our session.

"Not very well," Maria answered, and I could see that she was concerned. "I have a little money that my grandmother left me, and I do some waitressing and teaching, but it's not going to be enough to carry me through the six months of courses I have to take."

"Will you ask your father to help you?"

"I don't know. My father doesn't approve of my doing social work. He doesn't think it will pay enough."

Maria looked so glum that I decided to give her some perspective by sharing the experience I had had with my father.

"I felt a lot of guilt when I didn't do what my father wanted. When I decided to leave the brokerage business, I knew he was disappointed because he was hoping I would work for him. I had a hard time explaining why I wanted to get out of the rat race. Although I don't think he meant to, he made me feel very inadequate."

"I guess a lot of people have this problem," Maria commented.

"Yes," I replied, "I come across it often. The best we can do is to be true to ourselves and hope that others will learn to accept us." I gave Maria a sympathetic look.

She nodded her head in agreement. She was still very subdued. I decided to return to what I thought was the basis for her feeling so gloomy.

"I'd guess one reason why you're anxious about planning your job income is that it reminds you of the money issues you had with your parents over your previous jobs."

"Well, I wasn't actually thinking of them, but we did have a lot of arguments," Maria admitted. "I never wanted to do the planning they wanted me to."

I felt sad for Maria. Like many children, she had been turned off managing money because her parents had given her no meaningful purpose for doing it except to gain material wealth, although she could see that achievement wasn't making her parents happy. I decided to offer Maria another purpose which could inspire her to make her plan.

"It's perfectly normal to feel that way," I began. "I felt just as negative as you about managing until I realized I had a greater purpose for doing it than just making money."

"What was that?" Maria asked.

"Having peace of mind. Unlike you, I tried to do what my father wanted me to, but it caused me too much stress. I found myself worrying about stocks and bonds and not caring enough for my family or myself. I made plenty of money, but it didn't make me happy or secure. So I quit the brokerage business, moved to Maine, and learned to survive on much less money." I laughed ruefully at this thought.

"It must have been difficult to change your life style," commented Maria.

"Actually it wasn't," I replied. "I was so much happier not having the pressures of the business. That's when I recognized the importance of managing my finances. I had no choice but to plan them, but it was worth it to gain my independence."

"I can see how it would be," Maria replied, and I felt that she genuinely appreciated what I had done.

"It is for anyone who wants to reduce his or her money anxieties. As soon as I got a handle on my situation, I felt so much more in control of my life, and the process turned out to be quite transformative."

"In what way?" Maria asked.

"It showed me the changes I could make to simplify my life. Creating my plan forced me to look at how I was spending my money, and I saw how I could reduce my spending and clutter. At first I didn't like the idea of setting up a plan

because I thought it might restrict me, but ironically I discovered it was a liberating experience as it freed me from
my greatest fear—overspending." I paused here and waited
for Maria's reaction.

She looked a little worried. "I'm afraid the plan won't
mean very much to me since my income will never be
enough to pay my expenses."

"Most people in your situation believe this, and it often
stops them from making a plan and receiving the money
they need. In your plan you have to be realistic and put in
your income requirements, even if they seem beyond your
immediate reach. By doing this, you tell the Universe what
you want. The Universe can't help you unless it knows a specific dollar amount. With this amount as a goal, you can
then set in motion the thinking and actions necessary to
attract it."

"You make it sound easy," Maria responded dubiously.

"I can't say it will be easy. But you can make it happen if
you really want it to. And with a plan it will be much easier
than without one. It's a way of focusing your money energy."

"What do I have to do?"

"First you write down and total all your necessary
monthly living expenses as well as your business expenses.
You can use the form I gave you (see p. 237). Using this total
as a guide, you plan how you will go about making the income you'll need."

Maria looked perplexed. "I'll need help on this," she said.

"I thought we would do this together as part of our sessions."

"Fine."

The rest of our session was spent identifying the items
that Maria would need to estimate. I was pleased that she
was willing to do her plan even though her heart wasn't in it.

After our meeting was over, I continued to think about
Maria. As I straightened up my desk in preparing to leave, I
reached down to close a small book that was lying open on

my desk. It was James Allen's *As a Man Thinketh*. I had been reading it while I was waiting for Maria and had just started a chapter called "The Thought-Factor in Achievement." Its first sentence spoke directly to the challenge Maria presented me:

"All that a man achieves and all that he fails to achieve is the direct result of his own thoughts."[7]

Unless I could help Maria change her thinking toward money, she wouldn't achieve success in managing, no matter how much planning she did.

*   *   *

Whereas Maria had problems planning her job income, Tom had trouble looking at his!

TOM

Tom came to me because he needed $5,000 to pay off the surgeon who had operated on his wife. She had had cancer, and he had used up his available funds paying her other medical bills.

Before we got started, I asked Tom if he had reviewed his finances to see if he could come up with any additional money. He confessed that he got so depressed thinking about his finances that he had never gone over them. I suggested it was a good place to begin, so we examined his facts.

At first, I didn't see where Tom could get any money. He had only $200 in his checking account, no savings or investments, a house that was fully mortgaged, three personal loans from family members, several bank loans, and two credit cards that were at their limit.

I was just about to suggest that he consider bankruptcy when I took a second look at his monthly gross and net pay. His gross was $3,015 and his net was $1,966. I subtracted the net from the gross and found that his total salary deductions were $1,049 per month. That was a lot of money, and I decided to see what these deductions were. When I did, I found the dollars Tom was looking for.

Reviewing the income tax deducted from his paycheck and his estimated tax liability, I discovered that Tom could generate $1,500 by changing his exemptions and reducing his withholding tax. He could do this safely because he had so many medical expenses which could be deducted from his income that his taxes were going to be much less than he had estimated.

I also learned that Tom could get $700 from his company's voluntary savings plan. For more than a year he had been deducting $50 from his paychecks. It was a plan the employer had offered him when he had started with the company, and he had completely forgotten about it.

Along with the savings plan, Tom had elected to deduct another $50 to his company's stock option plan. We called the company and found that Tom owned $1,850 worth of company stock, which he could sell.

During the conversation with the company treasurer, we learned that Tom had an interest in a company pension fund worth $5,000, which he could borrow against up to $2,500 without any credit requirements.

When we totaled all these funds, we came to $6,550. This was money Tom didn't know he had, and he was a different person when he walked out of my office.

*   *   *

Though we have to pay some homage to our job income, we can't let it dominate our soul. Making sure our soul is in control is a continual challenge. Our self-centered natures are always pressing for more income—often to the detriment of our conscience.

This was vividly illustrated in the case of a woman who

called to tell me that she was getting a lawyer to force the courts to dock her ex-husband's paycheck. She was furious because he had refused to buy her daughter clothes even though he earned twice as much money as she did.

I listened to her while she let off steam. When she calmed down, I asked her how she was getting along with her ex-husband. I knew she had been making a Herculean effort to work with him since they shared six young children, and she felt that she needed his cooperation for the psychological well-being of the kids.

She answered that they were doing okay, except that he never paid his share of the costs. I said, if you take him to court, he'll blow up (I knew he had a very short fuse) and there will be a permanent rift in the family. I asked her if she were willing to live with that possibility.

She thought over what I said and decided that the rift would hurt the kids too much. But she didn't know how she could get the money. I suggested she talk to the ex-husband's parents and ask them to put pressure on him. She liked that idea as she had a good relationship with his parents and was sure they would try to help her. She ended the call by thanking me for the suggestion and helping her "keep her cool!"

When we are confronted with frustrations in dealing with others over paychecks, it is easy to let ourselves find solutions in combative action, such as the one proposed by this woman. Yet these actions always create more anger and pain. Thus before we do anything, we need to look in our hearts and decide what is the right thing for us to do. By doing what is right, we avoid self-recriminations and rifts which can last a lifetime.

Sometimes these decisions are too hard for us, and we can't make them. A student confessed that she had no trouble creating and following her plan when she was alone, but when she was living with her partner she couldn't follow it because she would spend so much of her money in supporting him. Even though she knew it wasn't good to foster his dependency, she couldn't bring herself to give him an ultimatum. I suggested that they do some counseling together, but she didn't think he would accept it. We agreed that her best solution was for her to work on getting stronger.

In thinking back on this interview, I was struck by the student's acceptance of herself. She admitted her weakness without guilt or recrimination. She saw it as being part of who she was, and though she wanted to change, she wasn't impatient or unrealistic in going about it. Eventually she was able to say no to her partner, and he was able to respect her decision.

Her frame of mind is what we all need when we are confronting concerns about our paychecks. Before we act, we need to identify where and why we have the frustration and then patiently work it out without chastising ourselves. When we fail to examine our feelings with honesty and compassion, we often sabotage ourselves by acting irrationally.

FAYE

Sometimes our examination forces us into a painful reassessment. It did for a woman named Faye who left a successful, high-paying promotion job in the South to come to Santa Fe, New Mexico. Faye found a husband in Santa Fe, but no job. Though her husband was working as an independent contractor, he wasn't earning enough money to support the two of them, and when they came to see me, they were planning to move to Berkeley, California, where they thought they could both get work.

In our session I learned that Faye had received $200,000 when she left her previous job, and there was only $30,000 left. She had no college degree and no experience in anything but promoting. Yet, because Faye had had such a good job, she felt she should be able to get a similar one in another field. She had tried and failed in Santa Fe and now was starting to repeat the process in Berkeley.

To compound her problems, she had been spending her savings as if she were employed in a high-paying job. Now she calculated that they had only a year left before her savings would run out. Yet, knowing this didn't dampen Faye's will to spend, and she had signed a lease for $1,400 per month on a house and office in Berkeley, even though neither of them had jobs there.

Normally when I am forced to bring people into reality, I try to be as gentle as possible. But in this case I knew I had to be brutally honest to get the message home.

I told Faye that she was overvaluing herself. Without a college degree in a sophisticated, high-priced place like Berkeley she would have little chance of getting a job that would cover her share of the rent and living costs. I predicted the couple would be on the streets and their dreams of having a happy marriage with children would never materialize if she continued to look for unrealistic jobs and to live beyond her means.

Faye didn't like what I said, and I could see the rebellion on her face. She had put a $2,000 deposit on the house in Berkeley and didn't want to lose it. I suggested she share the house and rent with others until they could earn enough income to cover the cost themselves.

I warned Faye that she should get any job she could in Berkeley. Even if she had to be a waitress, she should take it until a better job opened up. She couldn't afford to be unemployed. Once they both had paychecks to cover their living expenses, she should consider going back to college and getting her degree. Then she'd be qualified for the kind of job she wanted.

Faye tried to give me reasons why she didn't have to do what I asked, but I held my ground. Fortunately, her partner supported everything I said.

Several weeks later I got a call from her telling me she'd gotten a couple to share the rent in Berkeley and had found a friend in advertising who would hire her at $15,000 a year. The job didn't pay much, but she thought it had good potential. Her partner was going to work for a firm in San Francisco. His pay would be less than what he got as an independent contractor, but he could start earning money as soon as they moved.

She admitted that what I had said had been very painful, but it had helped her see the truth of her situation. She felt they would be okay now.

The only measure I have for my job income is whether or not it pays for my needs. If it does, fine. If it doesn't, I have to consider changing jobs or finding a way to make more money in my job. What really matters is not the job or the income, but how I approach my work. If I do it according to my highest principles, I know I'm making the most of myself.

Exercises:

1. Review your job income, deductions, and benefits including: federal, state, and city tax deductions; social security; medical and life insurance; retirement payments and benefits; and all other payments and benefits.

2. Review your monthly expenses. Compare them to your job income to see if you are living within your means. If you aren't, adjust your income and/or your expenses to bring them into line. If the job doesn't pay you enough to live on, consider changing jobs or adjusting your work to get more pay.

3. Evaluate the stress in your job. Is it worth what they are paying you? If not, consider changing jobs.

4. Evaluate the purpose of your job. Is it spiritually meaningful to you? If not, how can you make it so?

5. Evaluate the spiritual purposes you are manifesting in your job. Are you applying your spiritual ideals to your job? If not, why not? Example: If you are assigned to estimate the costs of a project, ask yourself if you are using persistency in getting all the cost details.

6. Before you take any job, take time to consider if it really feels right for you. If you have doubts, make sure they are resolved before you take the job.

7

Maintaining Your Center

Home Costs

I LEARNED that people have much more incentive to manage their home costs when they think of these costs metaphorically as a means of discovering their center. Our homes are images of ourselves, and we need to buy or rent the space that will help us be "at home" with ourselves. We may want to live in a loft, a mobile home, a river boat, a big city apartment, or a conventional suburban house. It doesn't matter which home as long as it reflects the essence of who we are.

Buying, selling, renting, or building homes can provoke a lot of money anxiety. To help those who have these fears, I have them look at their home costs in the context of their total financial picture. In most cases this review relieves them of the major worry of not knowing how much they can afford on their home by giving them dollar boundaries to work in.

Sometimes people find that they are overspending and have to find cheaper quarters. Decisions of this sort are never easy, but people are willing to make them when they understand the peace of mind their choices can bring.

MARIA'S SIXTH SESSION

In this session I planned to begin looking at Maria's expenses—specifically her home costs. But before I did, I decided to share two dreams I had the night before. They seemed so appropriate to our work.

As we sat down I started right in. "Maria, I'd like to share a couple of dreams I had last night. They may help us understand why we have so much trouble dealing with our finances."

"That sounds interesting," Maria replied. "I like dreams."

"In the first dream I saw myself as a child sitting in a phone booth crying and saying into the phone, 'Daddy, I don't want to be a businessman.' In the second, which came right after the first, I pictured my father giving me money. I was elated with the gift until he started complaining that I didn't appreciate him. Then I felt crushed and didn't want the money. I woke up feeling terribly sad."

I had Maria's full attention so I continued.

"I think the dreams are trying to help me understand my frustrations in dealing with money. The first dream seems to tell me that the child inside me doesn't want to be a businessman. The scene in the telephone booth is particularly appropriate as a backdrop for giving this message, since in my early years as a broker I spent most of my time on the phone creating my business. Though I was good at it, I didn't like it."

Maria seemed impressed. "That was a powerful dream," she said.

"Yes, it was," I replied, "and the second dream was powerful, too. It was almost like an explanation of the first. It showed me the paradox I had to live with in dealing with money. On the one hand I loved receiving it, but on the other hand I hated the emotional blackmail that went along with it."

"Was your father really like that?"

"Not really, though he did on occasion complain about our not appreciating him. That's why on a deeper level I think the second dream could be dramatizing an inner conflict within myself—the grown-up father in me trying unsuccessfully to bribe the child in me to accept the money world."

"I see what you mean."

"Both dreams forced me to look at my childhood attitude toward money. When I was growing up, business was not the family preoccupation it is now. We didn't have credit cards and couldn't buy so many things. The suburbia I lived in was still rural, and we were closer to nature. Money wasn't discussed, and there was a tacit distrust of it. Having too much and spending too much were frowned upon. We focused much more on human values than dollar values.

"This all changed, of course, from the late fifties on, when we as a nation had the war behind us and put all our energy into producing goods and services. During that time I watched my father get deeper and deeper into business until he almost drowned in it. I think many people did. Our generation had the benefit of living in both worlds, and I, for one, felt much happier in the simpler world. I find the highly competitive material world we live in today very unnerving. The child in my first dream obviously didn't like it either," I laughed.

Maria had been listening silently as I explained my history. After I finished, she said, "My parents have always been caught up in materialism."

"They grew up in the sixties and weren't exposed to the kind of world I was," I replied. "They lived during our biggest expansion years when money was getting a stranglehold on our values."

"It took over theirs," Maria said, a little bitterly.

"You can't blame them. They were just caught in the craze. People got so consumed in making money, and it seemed like so much fun in the beginning, they didn't see how it was going to hurt their spirit."

Maria sat in silence looking a little uncomfortable. I guessed the memories of the struggles with her parents were running through her mind. Her next words confirmed it. "It made my parents very competitive," she commented.

"Yes, and insecure. The more they have, the more they feel they need. They're never satisfied."

"Amen," Maria agreed.

I continued: "At some level they know material things and money don't fulfill their soul. But they've gotten so ensconced in their materialistic thinking they forget. I don't fault them. It's very easy to do."

I fell into silence. I thought I'd said enough about Maria's parents for the moment and wanted to bring the conversation back to Maria. Then I suddenly remembered the hippie movement of the sixties when hundreds of young people rebelled against the business establishment and formed communities based on love instead of money. Unfortunately their love couldn't sustain them or the movement. I knew that Maria would be familiar with the movement and, since she was rebelling in a similar manner, I felt she could learn from their experience. I began again.

"Most of your generation has caught the same dis-ease as your parents, but many, like yourself, find it so painful that you rebel against it like the hippies did in the sixties. They're a good example of how idealistic thinking can fail to sustain itself."

"Do you think the hippie movement failed?" Maria asked.

"Pretty much. Their communities weren't sustainable."

"Why?"

"One reason was that the followers of the movement didn't have their feet on the ground. They believed their ideals alone could change the world, and they weren't willing to deal with people and money in real ways."

A picture of the hippies dancing their celebration of freedom flashed in my mind. The thought of them poring over their finances made me chuckle.

"I don't think many of them looked at their financial picture or considered what other people's money situations were."

"I'm sure they didn't," Maria agreed.

"I think applying spiritual ideals successfully to living requires a lot of practical money thinking, and they weren't willing to do that. They also put their energy into the movement without first working on themselves. It seems to me the only way to change our 'bottom line' way of living is for each of us to get our own finances in order so that we won't be driven by fear in our decision making."

"So fear is our real problem?"

"I think so. It's our fear of not having enough that drives us to want to make more. Of course, that's only symptomatic of our deeper fear for our personal security." I stopped and tried to think of an example. I had just read about company executives getting millions of dollars in salaries, so I used that. "If it weren't that kind of fear, why would a company president need a $2 million salary? It's so irrational."

"It sure is," Maria agreed, nodding her head.

"If company presidents examined their expenses the way you're going to do, I think they'd see that they didn't need anywhere near that amount to live on, and they'd feel much more secure about their finances and their life in general."

Maria again nodded in assent. This time she looked a little apprehensive.

"I don't think I'm going to be secure looking at my expenses."

"You may not at first. But once you see how you can use the information as a guide for managing, you'll feel more confident."

"Okay, let's start."

Maria gave me her home costs. They included rent, heat (electricity), water, trash and sewer, and telephone. She had no maintenance or home insurance.

"Okay, here's your list of monthly home costs." I showed her the numbers on the worksheet. "The total comes to $394."

"That doesn't sound bad."

"It's not. Particularly for Santa Fe."

"How much is your monthly income?"

"I have about $4,000 to last me the next six months."

"Let's see, dividing six months into $4,000, I get about $667 per month. Subtracting your home costs from this amount gives you only $273 to cover your other monthly expenses. That doesn't seem like enough."

"No, it doesn't," Maria agreed, as she looked at my calculations.

"You'll have to get more money, but we can't tell how much until we see the rest of your expenses."

I put the list of Maria's home costs aside. As I did, I realized I hadn't asked her how she liked where she lived. "Do you like your living situation?" I asked.

"Yes," she replied.

"That's good. I think one's home is often the outward manifestation of who we are."

"Yes, I guess it is." Maria paused, and I could see she was mulling over my words. She then said: "I hadn't thought of it like that."

I decided to explain what I meant. "I often compare one's home to one's inner center. It's our safe space, and we need to be sure it's the right one for us."

Maria looked thoughtful. "In that case I'll have to pay more attention to my home," she said and grinned.

"And your home costs," I replied, smiling. "You'll need to watch them carefully to make sure you're comfortable with them also."

On those words our meeting ended.

* * *

GETTING A LANDLORD

When Maria rented her home, she was embarking on the spiritual challenge of working with a landlord. Whether we're tenants or landlords, we have the task of applying our spiritual ideals to the relationship. Yet often this isn't easy when money concerns interfere.

I had a case where a young student at the academy got caught in a bind with her landlord because her rent turned out to be more than she bargained for.

VICKI'S CASE

Vicki was renting a house from her stepfather, Jackson. Jackson had gone away for a year's sabbatical and had let Vicki stay in the house at a low rent with the understanding that she would maintain his place. Her mother talked her into accepting the offer which Vicki was reluctant to do since she didn't get along with Jackson. Once she moved in, she found she couldn't afford the expenses. She was on the verge of leaving when she decided to talk to me about it.

We reviewed her monthly expenses, including her home costs, and realized that she couldn't afford to stay unless Jackson was willing to pay his share of the maintenance costs. Vicki didn't think it would do any good to try to negotiate with her stepfather since they had so much trouble communicating.

I advised Vicki that it was much better for her to try to

come to terms with Jackson before leaving his house. Although she could legally leave without telling him because she had no written agreement, I thought it would undermine her integrity since she had promised to stay in the house while he was gone.

I remembered paraphrasing Edgar Cayce's advice to a client who complained bitterly about her mother. Cayce had said that the mother had complaints about the client also, but that it was up to the client to be kind and loving to the mother despite their differences. By the same token I said that it was up to Vicki to work out her rental differences with her stepfather even though she disliked him.

Vicki accepted my advice, but wasn't sure how she should go about the negotiation. I suggested that she show Jackson both the costs for living in his home and her own financial facts. Once he understood her situation, I thought that he might offer some concessions. I suggested that Vicki offer to do some work in exchange for his financial contribution.

Vicki presented her case and was surprised at how accommodating Jackson was. Though at first he was resistant, when he understood what Vicki was up against, he was willing to negotiate. They made an agreement that Vicki would paint the living room and bedroom and insulate the attic. In return, Jackson would pay for the materials and anything above $25 per month for the maintenance.

Ironically, in recounting to me the details of the agreement, Vicki left out the one request that might have helped her avoid taking on too many costs in the first place—that Jackson give her a written lease with all the terms!

Often landlords and tenants have much more difficulty ironing out their differences than Vicki and Jackson did. When these troubles arise, both parties need to search in their hearts for equitable ways of solving disputes. In most cases honest communication and the sharing of financial facts are real catalysts for coming to agreements.

GETTING A MORTGAGE LENDER

Though we don't have a landlord to contend with when buying a home, we usually have to deal with a mortgage lender, a situation which can be equally traumatic! Getting a mortgage often involves lots of patience and perseverance—two character-building traits.

To overcome our fears we need to have faith and real understanding of our financial facts, as I learned from a couple named Keith and Sharon who were searching for a mortgage.

KEITH AND SHARON

A year before I met them, Keith and Sharon had made the decision to move to the country and build a home. They had borrowed from friends and family to finance the construction. The house was built into the side of a hill. Keith built the house himself. He had just about completed it, when one of the friends who had lent him money asked to be paid back. Since they didn't have any extra money, they had to look for a mortgage.

Keith and Sharon applied to a mortgage bank, but got no response. At the time they made their application, interest rates were running about 13%, and it was very hard to find any mortgage money. They went to their local branch bank where they had an account, and the bank officer assured them that the bank would give them a mortgage. They waited several months and heard nothing from the officer. Finally he called and told them the bank wouldn't give them a loan.

That's when they came to me for help. As I listened to their story, I was impressed with the faith they had. They were Quakers who really believed the Universe would take care of them, and despite their two setbacks they were sure they could get a mortgage.

I was far from convinced. The house was unconventional with a garden on the roof, and most banks didn't like to give mortgages on these kinds of houses since it was impossible to get an accurate appraisal. Money was very tight, and many banks didn't have funds to lend out even at rates of 13% or more. Neither Keith nor Sharon had job security as they were both self-employed; Keith as a carpenter and Sharon as a tutor. Moreover, they had three young children and only $3,500 monthly income to support them. To me the chances of their getting a mortgage seem impossible.

However, buoyed by their optimism, I called a mortgage banker who had been referred to me and asked her if she had any mortgage money. To my surprise she said she did. She had some FHA (Federal Housing Administration) guaranteed mortgage money that she could lend at 12% interest. I asked her if we could come in the next day and apply for it, and she agreed.

I turned to the couple and told them the good news. However, I explained that although FHA-guaranteed mortgages don't have as tough requirements as regular bank mortgages, they had to convince the loan officer they could afford the loan, and to do this they needed to draw up a detailed picture of their finances.

I wrote down their figures, and they were better than I thought. Although they had very little available money, they had $30,000 of equity in their home. Most of this equity came from the labor Keith had put in. Their bank had appraised the house at $85,000. Given their equity, I thought it was possible they could get a mortgage of $40,000.

We reviewed their monthly income and expenses and found that if they reduced their workshops, entertainment, and gifts, they could just afford the $406 monthly payment on a $40,000 thirty-year mortgage. However, I thought they would be cutting it too close and should only go for a $30,000 mortgage. I felt that they needed to be conservative since they had such a bare-bones budget.

They reluctantly agreed, and the next day we went to see the loan officer. She was very impressed at the thumbnail sketch we had drawn up of Keith's and Sharon's finances. It was much more detailed than the form the bank required. However, when she reviewed Keith's income, she found that there was an error in his calculations, and Keith had over-estimated his income. Fortunately, it didn't make any difference since there was still enough monthly income between the two of them to cover the mortgage payments and their monthly expenses. On this basis the loan officer told Keith and Sharon that they could get the mortgage.

Later on as I reviewed the circumstances of this case, I realized that it was Keith's and Sharon's faith that galvanized me to make that phone call to the mortgage banker, and it was the financial picture that convinced the banker to lend the money. Yet the couple might have lost their chance for the mortgage if they had gone for the $40,000 loan instead of the $30,000 one, since the monthly income adjusted for the error was not enough to pay for the larger loan!

Dealing with a mortgage doesn't have to be a scary experience if we have the faith to go after it and understand our financial facts well enough to know exactly what we can afford.

GETTING A BUILDER

If we decide to build a home, we're faced with the daunting proposition of not only dealing with mortgages, but construction loans and builders. These don't need to overwhelm us if we are willing to confront them. Yet too often our egos block us from doing so. They take over and lead us into spending more money than we budget.

One time I was budgeting the construction costs for a client who had no perspective or control of her money. I told her that she could only afford $150,000 on her home, although I knew that she could really afford $200,000. In the end she spent $210,000, and I thought it was a victory that she held herself to that amount.

The most effective way to hold back our egos is to constantly review the building costs and our funds as we go along. These facts can be the catalyst for maintaining our personal and financial integrity.

On a deeper level our failure to confront the financial realities of building a home can be a form of self-denial. I had a good example of this in which the consequences of the individual's denial provided a painful but necessary reality check. I was having lunch with Wayne, a prosecuting lawyer, and we were talking about the need for forgiving others who short-changed us on business deals. He confessed he was having a hard time forgiving his builder who had been a good friend. In fact, he was thinking of suing him.

I asked Wayne to tell me what had happened, and he did. He had a fixed contract with this builder named Eric for $120,000 and got a construction loan for that amount for six months. Eric started building in the middle of winter two months after the loan was authorized. Wayne had no idea why the delay, but now, thinking back on it, he realized that it should have been a warning.

During the construction Wayne and his wife periodically went out to see what was happening. Neither of them could understand why there wasn't more being done, but every time Wayne's wife tried to talk about it, Wayne denied there was a problem. He assumed his friend was doing his best. Eventually he resisted getting out of his car to look at the site because he didn't want to see what was happening.

With two weeks to go the builder called and said that he couldn't complete the house as he had run out of money. He needed an additional $10,000. He complained that lumber prices had gone up, and he had underestimated his finishing costs.

Even though under the contract the builder was responsible for these costs, Wayne felt that he had to pay them since, if he didn't, the builder couldn't complete the house and Wayne would lose his mortgage loan, the house, and ten acres of land which he had purchased outright.

Wayne agreed to the payment with the understanding that the builder would pay all the subcontractors off so that there would be no possibility of having liens on the property.

When a week later Wayne found a $4,000 lien on the property filed by the electrician, he fired his friend as he realized that he had been lying to him about how he had spent his money. The house looked just about completed. However, when he moved in, he found the living room needed plastering, the cabinets were not completed, the floor had air pockets in it, and there was exposed wiring. To top it off, the builder had failed to pay several of the other subcontractors.

After hearing this story, I told Wayne that I understood completely why he had difficulty forgiving the builder. I asked him what he would have done differently if he had the chance.

He said that he would have first checked with the construction industry division to see what kind of record the builder had. Then he would have talked to the people who had used him to build their homes instead of merely looking at the pictures of the homes in the builder's portfolio.

"Then I would have policed the builder's spending and construction much more carefully," Wayne added. "I never even looked at the builder's expenses before giving the bank permission to pay him my loan money." Wayne shook his head in disbelief.

"But your intention was right. He was your friend and you trusted him," was all I could think of to console him.

"That's true," Wayne replied, "but it doesn't take away the pain. What makes it even worse, I didn't write in the contract the basic protection clauses I would automatically write in for my clients. I didn't even make a provision requiring the builder to pay the legal costs," Wayne grimaced.

"It might help to look at why this happened to you."

"I've been wondering why," Wayne looked at me pensively.

I thought of what I knew about Wayne. He always seemed to me to be living in a world of his own. I felt that he enjoyed that world much more than the world he was actually living in. I had known others, including myself, who suffered from this escapist syndrome.

"It may have to do with your wanting to avoid dealing with the practical realities of life," I said. "I know you go off on many retreats. I suspect you find them much more fulfilling than dealing with your builder," I laughed.

"I do," Wayne replied.

"I find that when I try to retreat from life that it doesn't let me get away with it. Maybe you're being told that you need to be more in this world."

"You're right. But I think I should have been more honest with myself."

"It would seem so. You didn't take care of yourself in this deal."

"I certainly didn't."

"Well, you had a very painful reality check. If I were you, I might sue the builder just to affirm myself and my willingness to be in this world." As an afterthought I said, "Yet one hates to sue a friend."

"He's no longer my friend," Wayne said sadly.

"That's the worst loss of all," I replied.

*   *   *

This case reminded me that no matter how "spiritual" we'd like to be, we can't be blind to our human weaknesses. When building a home, we have to not only watch our egos, but our builders!

Whether we are renting, buying, or building a home, the

process is akin to the spiritual process of finding our spiritual center—that special space where we can be at peace with ourselves.

Emmanuel in *Emmanuel's Book*, compiled by Pat Rodegast and Judith Stanton, describes this metaphysical search very well:

"You have come to traverse a wide terrain of experience in order to verify where truth lies and where your distortion is in that terrain. You will then be able to return to your home center, your soul-self refreshed and wiser."[8]

On the practical, financial level, an important part of our search for a physical home is making sure our home costs are in line with our finances. If they aren't, we won't find the security we are looking for.

* * *

Exercises:

1. *When renting a home,* review your available funds and your required rental deposits.

    Review your monthly rental costs, including rent, heat, electricity, water, trash and sewer, and any maintenance required.

    Compare your total monthly costs to your monthly income.

    Before making your rental decision, meditate on it. If you have doubts, don't sign the lease.

2. *When buying a home,* review your available funds and your down payment.

    Review the terms of your mortgage.

    Review your closing costs.

    Review the monthly costs for owning your home, including mortgage payment, heat, electricity, water, trash and sewer, maintenance, taxes, and insurance.

    Compare the total monthly costs to your monthly income.

    Before buying a home, meditate on your decision. If you have doubts, hold off on the purchase.

3. *When building a home,* have an architect or builder draw up detailed plans.

    Get two or more bids from builders.

    Review your available funds and monthly income and expenses.

    Go to a lender and find out if the project is financially realistic.

    Before going forward with the project, meditate on it. If you have any doubts, hold off until you are sure it is right for you.

    Get an appropriate construction loan that you can convert into a mortgage.

While the construction goes on, review the builder's expenses and the progress of his work before authorizing the lender to make progress payments to the builder. Make sure everything is completed before making a final payment.

Review the terms of the mortgage.

Buying or building a home is a complicated business. I have given you only the most essential exercises. You need to review the procedures with an expert before starting these projects.

8

Furthering Your Journey

Car Costs

THE SIGNIFICANCE of managing car costs was brought home to me in a report by a student named Katie. I had asked her to write about an experience that had affected her attitude toward managing money. Here is what she wrote:

KATIE'S REPORT

"At the age of forty-two, after years of avoiding the issue, I was forced by circumstances to really deal with my financial situation. I had become single after twenty-two years of marriage. I had two of my children still at home and had recently returned to the work force. My job was twenty miles from home. I owned two cars; one didn't run and the other was rapidly losing its transmission.

"I was extremely fearful—afraid that I wouldn't know how to take the necessary steps to buy a car, certain no one would ever loan me money, certain no one would give me anything for my old cars, and afraid to really look at how much money I had available.

"I could see no way out. Since I could no longer turn to someone else to take care of me, I had to take responsibility for myself.

"The acts of examining my resources carefully and deciding what I could afford, shopping for a car, reaching an agreement with a car dealer, and filling out the loan application were very powerful for me. The day I drove my new car home was the first time I had ever felt like an independent adult—a real grown-up! I no longer felt that the whole subject of money was too fearful to deal with. I had discovered that I could make the system work for me if I faced it and followed a step-by-step process."

Katie's report woke me up to the personal power one can gain through managing car costs. For her it was an important step on her life's journey.

Most of us feel a special relationship to our car. It's our friend and companion, and how we manage its costs has important psychological and spiritual implications for us.

When I was growing up, the car was like a family emblem. We'd have endless conversations about how well it was going, how it compared with others, and what we had to do to take care of it. Now I see we were treating the car as if it were an extension of ourselves; and in evaluating how well it was going, we were also evaluating how well we were going.

I had read that in dreams the car was often a symbol for the dreamer's body; and one time, when I was totally exhausted, I had a dream that our car had a flat tire and my wife, Leila, was helping me change the tire. After we talked about the dream the next day, I felt sure that the car was a symbol for me, the flat tire a symbol of my being flattened, and the message was that I needed Leila's help to get my strength back.

In another dream I saw a friend of mine backing her car out of her garage, and I knew the scene represented her course of action. She was backing out of a commitment she had made with me.

Whether we think of our car from a practical or a psychological viewpoint, it has an enormous impact on our lives. Recognizing this should give us the impetus to manage our car costs. Unfortunately in many cases it doesn't, as our money fears get in the way.

When I consult with people, I help them examine their car concerns within the context of their financial facts. As is so often the case in this work, it's not the money or the car that is the issue. It's the attitude of the owner.

Before my seventh session with Maria, I told her that we were going to talk about her car costs. To make our discussion more meaningful, I decided to consider the costs in conjunction with four spiritual practices that would help her overcome her management anxieties. I got these practices from Eknath Easwaran's book called *Meditation*.[9] The practices include meditating, slowing down, giving one-pointed attention, and training the senses.

MARIA'S SEVENTH SESSION

I started the session by asking Maria if she had ever heard of Eknath Easwaran.

"Yes, I have," she replied. "He's the spiritual man from India who taught at Berkeley."

"That's right. Have you read his book called *Meditation?*"
"No."
"It's a good, down-to-earth book on how to live a spiritual life. You might want to read it. I mention it because it has four spiritual practices which I recommend everyone use in his or her financial decision making."
"What are they?" Maria asked.
"Meditating, slowing down, giving one-pointed attention, and training the senses," I replied.
I was about to go on when Maria stopped me.
"Wait a minute. I'd like to write these down." She took a pencil and paper and copied the practices. "I like them, but I'm not sure how they apply to managing money."
"Since we're going to examine your car costs in this session, let me try to apply these steps to managing them."
"Okay."
"Let's start with *meditating.* I think it's helpful to meditate on any major financial decision, including one concerning your car."
Maria looked perplexed. "What do you mean by *meditating?*" she asked.
"Well, Easwaran suggests silently reciting a spiritual passage. However, for making financial decisions, I suggest taking a few moments to still the mind."
"That's a relief," Maria said. "I was afraid you were talking about levitating," she laughed.
"No, but if it could help me find my answers, I'd try it," I said, laughing back at her.
"What I'm suggesting isn't hard to do," I continued. "We do it when we look off in space, close our eyes, or just sit still for a moment."
"Sure, I've done that," Maria said.
"Well, if you do any of those things just before you make that final decision to buy a car, it can help you determine how you really feel about that car."
"How?" Maria asked.

"As you contemplate the car, you'll intuitively know if it feels right to buy it."

Maria considered this for a moment. "Does it always work?" she asked.

"Not always," I replied, "but the more I do it the better I get at assessing my feelings. I think I now can tell when it really feels right to do something."

"I'll have to try it," Maria said and rolled her eyes. "Meditating over my car; that's a new one," she laughed again.

"Why not," I said lightly, "if it calms your nerves, it'll be worth it." I paused and considered if I should say more. Since Maria seemed receptive to this intuitive approach, I decided to share another dream with her.

"You know, Maria, I once had a dream that helped me choose a car."

"You did?"

"Yes. The dream happened the night after we made a decision to look for a used car. In the dream I had just found a car to buy, and a good friend was laughing with me about how I could fix this car with chewing gum. I took the dream as a good omen, since my friend knew a lot about cars and was very successful with them. Using chewing gum implied the need for minimum maintenance. When, the next day, Leila found a car advertised in the papers that fit our exact needs, I had no hesitation about going after it. It turned out to be a great one."

"That was quite a dream," Maria remarked.

"It was," I replied, "and it made me realize that I can rely on my inner self in making decisions like this." I stopped there as I thought it was time to move on to the rest of practices.

"Let's look at the other three spiritual practices," I said.

"Okay," Maria answered.

"The next two I lump together since I find that they are interrelated when I apply them to managing money. *Slowing down* and *one-pointed attention*." I paused to give Maria a chance to take them in. Then I continued, "These are powerful tools because they help us concentrate our attention. In managing finances we can easily get overwhelmed by the details, but if we slow down and give them our total attention, we usually can make sense of them." I smiled at Maria. "You'll see this when we examine your car costs."

Maria grimaced. "I don't like looking at these costs."

"That's just the point," I interjected. "Most people don't, so they skip over them. Whenever I'm talking car costs to sales or service personnel, I always make them go over each cost very slowly so that I can focus on it. Giving each my full attention takes a lot of the fear out of the individual items."

"I get you," Maria said.

I paused here and turned to the next step.

"Now the last step is *training the senses*."

"What's that mean?" Maria asked.

"For Easwaran it means controlling our senses. Our senses are so programmed by our culture to want material things that they have to be trained to be discriminating."

Maria thought for a moment. "This would relate to controlling our spending."

"Exactly. We need to control the sensory impulses which lead us to buy items we can't afford or don't need.

"To use the car example again: when we are buying a car, if we let our senses control us, they will choose a car that's beyond our means. We need to curb these senses to get a car that we can afford."

"How do we do that?" Maria asked.

"Easwaran says that we should use meditation and our mind to control our senses," I said with a smile.

"That's a big assignment," Maria said, shaking her head.

"I know." I paused. It was true that relying on the mind alone wasn't enough for most people. They needed to know their money facts as well. It gave them boundaries to work in. I suggested this to Maria.

"I find that examining our financial facts is also effective.

Seeing the costs can keep us in reality."

"That will be another challenge for me," Maria said, taking in a breath.

"It won't be hard," I replied. I took out a pad and pencil. "Let's take a look at your car costs and see what we can make of them."

"Well, they're a little complicated since my mother owns my car," Maria said.

"Why's that?" I asked, putting the pencil and pad down.

"I inherited an old family car, and the insurance was so much cheaper if it was kept in her name," Maria replied.

"I understand. It's expensive to get insurance when you're under twenty-five," I said.

"It's awful!" Maria exclaimed.

"Who pays your insurance?" I asked.

"I did until recently. Now she does. I just can't afford it," Maria replied.

"What about the other costs?" I asked.

"I'm supposed to, but I don't think the car's worth keeping," Maria answered.

"What kind of car is it?" I asked.

"It's a 1984 Chrysler."

"What kind of mileage has it got?"

"About 150,000 miles."

"That's quite a few miles."

"I know. I was told it needs a lot of work."

"Have you talked with your mother about it."

"She won't listen to me. Every time I try to tell her I need a new car, she acts as if she doesn't hear me. She says the car is plenty good enough for me."

Maria looked down and was silent. I saw the disappointment on her face. I knew rejections like this usually aren't based solely on the condition of the car.

"Maybe the car isn't the issue," I said.

Maria didn't answer, but the look she gave me told me I was right.

"That's tough," I said, "but perhaps if you approach it from a business point of view, she might be more receptive. She cares a lot about money, and if she sees it's financially impractical to keep this car, she may be willing to make a change."

"That might work. She doesn't like losing money." Maria seemed encouraged by this idea.

"You might as well try. You have nothing to lose."

"Okay."

We spent the rest of the session working out the information Maria needed to give her mother.

In the following week I had Maria outline her average monthly car costs—gas, regular maintenance, and insurance—and get an estimate of what it would cost to get the Chrysler in reasonable shape. Maria took the car to the mechanic the family used, and he estimated the cost to be approximately $3,000.

I then suggested that Maria talk to the Chrysler dealer about getting a newer used car. The dealer told Maria she could get a similar 1988 Chrysler with 60,000 miles on it for about $2,000 if she traded in her old Chrysler just as it was. Maria was elated since this deal would be $1,000 cheaper than overhauling the 1984 car.

I showed Maria how to estimate the monthly costs of the 1988 Chrysler, and in comparing the costs of the two cars she found that she could save on average $20 in gas costs and $20 in maintenance by buying the 1988 model. This more than made up for the increase in insurance costs.

Maria took these facts to her mother, and when she saw them, she agreed to trade in Maria's 1984 car for the 1988 Chrysler. Although she wasn't happy about putting up the extra money, she realized the trade made economic sense.

"I was amazed," Maria said, when she told me of her mother's decision. "And the best part was I could see she respected me."

"Now you know the power of practical economics," I replied.

*   *   *

While the choice of whether or not to buy a car hinges to some extent on one's finances, it can just as much depend on one's priorities.

ROBIN

In a case I had several months ago a nurse named Robin was almost persuaded to buy a new car until she looked at her other expenses and discovered that her education was more important. It began when the Dodge service manager told Robin that her Dodge wasn't worth fixing. He offered, however, to exchange her Dodge at a good price if she bought a new one. Robin looked at the new Dodges and found one she liked, but before making the purchase, she came to me to see how she should finance it. With three kids to support, she knew it wouldn't be easy.

We examined her financial picture and the costs of getting a new car. We discovered that although she had enough savings to cover her registration, insurance, and other initial costs, she didn't have enough monthly income to cover her current monthly expenses plus her car loan payment.

In going over Robin's expenses, we found that she could afford the car payment if she gave up the course she was taking for her advanced nursing degree. However, Robin was loath to give up this course since it was important to her career.

I asked Robin if the Dodge service people had really gone over the old car to see if it was worth keeping. She said that she wasn't sure. They had told her that she needed a new transmission for $1,600, which sounded bad to her. I suggested that she get a second opinion on the condition of her car from a local mechanic.

A week later Robin did, and the mechanic told her that all the Dodge needed was to fix the transmission, and he could do it for $1,200. Robin called me with this news and her decision to hold on to her car.

"My degree is much more important than a new car," were Robin's words.

"Yes," I replied, "and once you get your degree, you'll be in a better position to get a raise, and then you could afford a new car."

Along with our priorities in buying a car, we have to consider our needs, goals, and state of mind. The latter is essential, since it can be the determining factor in whether or not we make the best financial deal.

Usually when we are shopping for a car, we are both excited and scared: excited at the prospect of getting something new, and scared by how much it will cost us and whether it will be a good choice. In this frame of mind we can easily fall prey to a salesperson who dazzles us with the more expensive models and cajoles us with the seemingly low loan costs. Since most of us are intimidated by the costs, we are more than willing to believe the quotes of the salesperson without examining what they really mean.

What we need to manage this transaction well is control, but our state of mind precludes us from having it.

To help people get this control, before they shop for a car, I have them look at the following facts:

a. the trade-in value of their present car (if they own one);
b. their savings and other available funds;
c. the down payment, registration, and other initial costs of buying a new car;
d. the monthly costs of having the new car (insurance, loan payment, gas, maintenance, parking, etc.);
e. their monthly income and expenses.

By comparing their trade-in value, savings, and other available funds to their down payment, registration, and other initial costs, they can see how much they can afford for the down payment on their new car; and by including their monthly costs for their new car in their summary of income and expenses, they can determine how much they can afford to pay on a monthly basis.

Armed with this information, I send them off to car dealers, and invariably they return with stories of having mastered the transaction. The reasons for their successes are obvious. They are neither scared nor overly excited since they have a realistic idea of what they can afford. As soon as they tell the salesperson the down payment and monthly loan payments they can pay, the seller obliges them by showing them cars in their price range. When the seller tries to persuade them to buy a car out of their range, they use their facts to keep them within their limits. In most cases their facts help them bargain for lower prices.

One older woman told me how she bargained for two cars with the same dealer to get the best car she could. In the first negotiations she traded in her "old klunker" for a 1991 used Honda. The dealer wanted $9,000, but the woman bargained the price down to $7,000 by telling him she couldn't afford to pay more than $179 per month on her car loan.

Several months later when the Honda was not performing well, the woman's son examined the car and made a list of all the car's defects. The woman took the list to the dealer and told him that she knew a lot of people in the community, and she knew they wouldn't approve of the dealer selling her a bum car, especially when she had had to use her social security money to buy it.

The dealer was embarrassed and offered to exchange her 1991 Honda sedan for a new 1993 Subaru stationwagon. The dealer tried to raise her monthly loan payment from $179 to $250, but the woman bargained the amount down to $220. Thus, for an additional $41 per month this woman got a brand-new, fully warranted car.

The woman did her bargaining alone and had no knowledge of cars or costs. Her ability to negotiate came from her understanding and adherence to her own financial facts.

I've found that we can gain the same kind of strength when we examine the financial facts of our daily car costs. Let's look at them.

Gas

I used to find myself always trying to get the cheapest price on gas, even to the point where I would make life-threatening turns on the highway just to get to the gas station offering the best deal. After a few close calls, I began to ask myself if it was worth the savings. I did the math to find out how much money I saved and discovered it was usually less than a dollar. For this amount it wasn't worth the risk, so I stopped doing it.

Subsequently I examined why I had been so determined to save on the price of gas, and I found that it was just a symptom of my anxiety about spending money. Looking at the cost savings helped me gain perspective on my fear.

Maintenance

Buying gas is not as traumatic as spending money on repairs. I know few people who want to pay the price for keeping their car in good condition. When Leila tells me there is something wrong with the car, my first instinct is to deny it, and then try to put off getting the car fixed for as long as possible. Though I hate to admit it, I know it's my fear of the cost which makes me act this way. To overcome this attitude, I try to keep to the maintenance schedule outlined in the manual. These facts help remind me of what has to be done.

In working with others who have anxieties over their car repair costs, I ask them to get one or more cost estimates for the work. Then I have them review these estimates in the context of their total financial picture (see summary, p. 237). This usually calms their nerves, as they see the reality of their money situation and how best they can pay for the repairs.

Car loan payments

When people come with concerns about these costs, I have them call the bank or car dealer to get the annual interest rate, the monthly payments, and the total costs of the loans for one to five years. Then they insert the loan payments into their financial picture (see summary, p. 237) to see which loan they can best afford. Having this information reduces their anxiety, since it gives them a sound dollar basis for deciding which loan, if any, to have.

Car insurance

Car insurance costs are formidable because they are expensive and complicated. The thought of shopping for car insurance is so intimidating that many people don't bother to compare prices, even though they know they might save money if they did.

To help people gain the courage to tackle these costs, I have them call the insurance agent or company and get the costs of the insurance. These costs include personal liability, collision, personal property, other benefit costs, and the total annual cost. They compare these to the costs of having comparable insurance with other companies. Then they examine the cost in the context of their total financial picture (see summary, p. 237) to see if they can afford it. In many cases these facts alone are sufficiently empowering to motivate people to manage their insurance.

Recently, I got two quotes from two highly rated insurance companies for a homeowner's policy that included car insurance. One was over $400 cheaper than the other, and both policies offered the same protection. Thus I know it's

worth our while practically as well as psychologically to get
the cost facts on this insurance.

Yet facts alone don't determine our behavior. I know a
forty-year-old farmer who drives around in a 1940 hot rod
even though she knows it costs too much to maintain. I've
tried to get her to buy a newer model but she refuses, because she wants to make up for the time during her
teen-age years when she was not allowed to have one of
these cars. Now as then she wants to be one of the "hot rod"
gang!

In another case involving peer pressure, a student in my
class reported that her father always bought the same
model car in the same price range because the family lived
in a small town, and he didn't want to draw attention to himself by buying a more expensive car. He had one of the better
jobs and could afford a more expensive car, but he was
afraid to show off his wealth.

Cases like these are only samples of the many human issues I found that affected people's car decisions. One I
appreciated most was the case of a retired pharmacist who
wanted to know if she should let her ex-husband buy her a
new car. She had a good relationship with him, and he could
afford to buy her one. He had recently bought their daughter a new car, and since his alimony payment was very low,
she felt she had plenty of justification for asking him.

I asked her how it made her feel to ask him for a new car,
and she said it didn't make her feel good as she never
wanted to be beholden to him.

I pointed out that a new car might cost as much as
$12,000, which was not a significant amount for her ex-hus-
band to pay. I asked her if she really needed a new car. She
said she wasn't sure, but the service man had said that she
had a major engine problem which would cost her about
$2,000 to repair.

"How many miles has the car gone?" I asked.

"About 60,000," she answered.

"In that case," I replied, "you might be better off fixing your car if there's nothing else wrong with it. I've driven several of the cars I've owned over 150,000 miles, and $2,000 is a lot more affordable than $12,000."

The retired pharmacist decided to keep her car, but asked if she should ask her husband to pay for the repairs.

Since I knew she could afford these repairs, I suggested that she not ask for them, but tell him about them and see if he offered to pay for them. If he did, she could accept his offer, but if he didn't, she could take care of them herself.

"In that way you will keep your self-respect," I concluded.

"Good idea," she replied. "I never want to lose that."

The issue in this case was not just about car costs but self-worth. When the retired pharmacist recognized this, she had no trouble making the right decisions.

Every financial decision has a spiritual dimension, and our task is to understand that dimension and use it as a guide.

To motivate ourselves to manage our car costs, I find it helpful to think of our car as part of ourselves and of our journey on this earth. If our car is not well maintained, we'll never get where we want to go.

* * *

Exercises:

If you own a car:

A. Write down the average monthly costs, including gasoline, maintenance, car loan payments, and insurance.
B. Examine how you manage these costs and identify the anxieties they cause you.
C. Review your insurance policy, including its liability and collision protection, personal property, and other benefits.
D. Review the terms of your car loan, including the annual interest, the monthly payments, and the total cost.
E. Have a mechanic evaluate the condition of your car. Get an estimate of any costs for repairing it.
F. Compare your average monthly costs on your current car with the monthly costs of owning a new car.
G. Meditate on how you feel about owning this car, and decide if it is the right car for you.

If you are buying a car:

Before making the purchase,

A. Get a cost sheet from the salesperson detailing the costs of the new car you'd like to buy.
B. Get an estimate of the trade-in value of your car, if you own one.
C. Compare the trade-in value with the outstanding balance of your current car loan, if you have one.
D. Calculate the down payment.
E. Calculate the loan you will need to buy a new car.
F. Find out the cost of the loan for one to five years and the monthly loan payments.
G. Find out the insurance costs on the new car.
H. Compare the average monthly costs—gas, mainte-

nance, insurance—of a new car with the current monthly costs of your old car, if you have one.

I. Insert your down payment and new monthly car costs into your financial picture (see p. 237) to see if the new car is financially right for you.

J. Look at your needs and the pluses and minuses of the new car. Ask yourself how it fits in with who you are and your stage of life.

K. Meditate on the purchase. If it feels right, go ahead with it. If there are any doubts, hold off until the doubts are gone.

9

Simplifying Your Life

Possessions

MOST PEOPLE don't realize that taking a financial inventory of their possessions is a way to take stock of themselves, but I find it provides another meaningful assessment of who we really are.

When we start out in life, our possessions are primarily reflections of our parents, since they gave them to us. But as we become independent and have the money and power to choose our own possessions, they become an image of ourselves.

Our clothes, furniture, paintings, car, TV, VCR, computer, etc., can be much more meaningful to us when we think of them as reflections of who we are and not just as physical items. This isn't hard to do, since many of our possessions show our interests and life style, direct manifestations of our thoughts and feelings. Since our thoughts create things, we have to monitor our thinking to make sure that the possessions we acquire are the most suitable for us.

Yet in my counseling I find that people usually don't consciously control what they own. They go from day to day buying things as if they can afford them without giving due deliberation to their needs and priorities. As a result, they often find themselves unconsciously accumulating more than they need or can afford. While these possessions may temporarily satisfy their egos, they often create more stress by cluttering up their lives and overextending their pocketbooks.

To help people gain perspective on their personal possessions, I ask them to write down a rough estimate of how much they are worth. Often this request floors them as they have no idea of their value. I give them estimates to work with—$1,000 to $3,000, $3,000 to $5,000, $5,000 to $10,000, $10,000 to $20,000; with these guidelines they can come up with an approximate figure. Then I ask them if they have any valuable items over $500—antiques, paintings, etc. If they have, I ask them to get an appraisal of the items and send the evaluation with or without a videotape to the insurance companies. This will give them the proof of value they need if they have to get reimbursed for loss or damage.

As we discuss the values of their possessions, I ask my clients about the stresses those possessions may create. Many complain that they have too many things, but haven't the will to sort them out. Sometimes just seeing the value of their possessions prompts them into action.

ROGER AND LOUISE

Such was the case with a couple named Roger and

Louise, but it was not without a struggle. The couple came to me because their marriage was being jeopardized by the stress of having too many debts. They had over $10,000 of credit card loans, and they were falling behind on their monthly payments. They had no savings and only minimum balances in their checking account.

Their arguments over how to manage these debts were a continual bone of contention. Roger thought that he should get another job, but Louise didn't want him to since she reasoned it would be an excuse for him to spend less time with her and their two children, aged eight and ten. Louise was frustrated with working only part-time, but didn't feel that she could manage a full-time job and take care of the children.

When I asked the couple to give me an estimate of the value of their personal possessions, Roger said "about $5,000." Louise then interjected, "But what about the furniture in the garage? It must be worth at least $2,- or $3,000."

Roger replied, "It doesn't belong to us. It's going to the kids."

I asked Roger to explain about this furniture. He said he had been given an antique desk and cabinet by his parents several years before they died. Louise hated the pieces and wouldn't have them in the house, so Roger kept them in the garage. He wanted to hold on to them for the kids.

"Do you know what they are worth?" I questioned.

"No, they were old family pieces we got when my parents went to the nursing home," Roger replied. "We never found out their value. My parents died several years ago and didn't leave any records on them."

I advised him to get an appraisal, if only for establishing a value for insurance purposes. Roger agreed, and we moved on to other subjects.

During the rest of the session we completed their financial picture and established how much additional income Roger and Louise needed to meet the monthly payments on their credit card loans. The meeting ended without their coming to any conclusion on how to get this additional income.

Several weeks later the couple returned. Now they were in a quandary as to what to do with Roger's desk and cabinet. They had gotten an appraisal from a well-known antique dealer, and he said the antiques were worth more than $20,000. They were original Chippendale eighteenth-century English pieces.

The appraisal created another issue. Roger still wanted to give them to the children, but Louise wanted to sell them and pay off their debts.

I sided with Louise, and told Roger I thought it was impractical to store such valuable furniture in their garage until their kids were old enough to use it. The cabinet and desk would need to be stored for about ten years; at best they would dry out and at worst be damaged. The couple didn't have the money to store them properly or insure them individually, and the home policy wouldn't cover their insurance.

Roger was still reluctant to sell. He felt an obligation to his parents to keep the furniture in the family. I pressed him to tell me more about his relationship to his parents and his feelings toward this furniture. He admitted that he had disappointed his parents a lot and that probably this guilt toward them was preventing him from acting sensibly about the antiques.

I asked Louise why she disliked the furniture, and she confessed that it reminded her of Roger's parents, whom she blamed for many of their marital problems.

As our discussion unfolded, we all realized that the cabinet and desk were symbols of Roger's parents and for that reason alone should be sold, since they were charged with negative emotions.

From a financial standpoint they both agreed that the sale would reduce a major stress in their marriage as their credit card loans were a big issue, and they could use the proceeds from the sales to pay them off. This would also mean that neither of them would have to change their work loads.

Finally, we agreed that the children would also benefit from the sale since there would be more peace in the family, and giving them peace was more important than giving them valuable antiques!

When I see people like Roger and Louise who need to get rid of possessions, I often exhort them to do so if only to simplify their lives. That would give them more time to focus on more meaningful aspects of life which, in the long run, would be much more rewarding than owning possessions. I often refer to Edgar Cayce's words in *Think on These Things,* "For the material, at best, is only temporal, or temporary, while that which may be builded from spiritual desire, spiritual purposes, is eternal."[10]

Too many possessions trap us in our material world, and we become possessive not only of things but of money. We start measuring ourselves by what we own in dollars and cents instead of by who we are as persons. We classify possessions by what they cost instead of what they mean.

Recently I went into an ardent collector's home, and my eyes were overwhelmed by the knickknacks that he had purchased for every wall and cranny. There were so many I couldn't appreciate any single item. In my mind I roundly criticized the collector for his lack of discrimination. Then I went home and discovered that I, too, had used precious dollars to clutter my home with too many things. I think many of us tend to spend too much energy on purchasing things and not enough energy on sorting them out.

Yet possessions are important if they add meaning to our lives. Beautiful antiques, paintings, and rugs can inspire us and help us appreciate creative ability and beauty. Nice clothes in moderation can lift our self-image; books can expand our thinking; and computers, our means of communication. There are many possessions which can enrich our lives, but we have to be selective to insure that they meet real needs, not ego-driven ones.

For those who really want to reduce their material stress, I ask them to take a separate inventory besides the financial one. It requires that they assess their possessions as to whether or not these provide a meaningful part of their lives. Invariably people find items they can get rid of, since so many of the possessions they own lose meaning over time.

I know one collector who has a strict rule. Every time he adds a piece to his collection, he has to get rid of another one. Thus he never increases the number of his items, and each one he acquires has to be more meaningful than the one he lets go.

Since there is such a temptation to overspend on possessions, doing a dollar evaluation can also be another way of controlling what we own, since it makes us aware of how much we are spending on material items.

For Maria it was another stepping-stone on her way to changing her money consciousness. In reviewing our previous sessions, I felt that Maria had made progress, and the last one on car costs had really shown her the power of practical economic thinking. However, to change her money consciousness, I knew that she needed to come to grips with some core beliefs about money. Since I planned to discuss her possessions and property in this session, the one belief that came to mind was prosperity.

MARIA'S EIGHTH SESSION

I began our session with a straightforward question:
"Maria, how do you feel about owning possessions?"
"Not great," she replied.
"Why?" I questioned.
"I don't know. I guess I'm just sick of all this material stuff.

I hate it when my mother tries to give me things. And she always harps on what I will inherit when she dies. It depresses me."

"When you were growing up, did your parents talk a lot about their possessions?" I asked.

"All the time," Maria replied. "And everybody else's. They were always comparing who had what, and how much it was worth, and where they could get the best bargains."

"Did they argue over their possessions?"

"Lots of times."

"Over what."

"Who should have them. Where they should go. How to take care of them. How much to pay for them. It was an obsession with them." Maria gave me one of her baleful looks.

I was silent. Her words prompted my memory of some of my father's discussions about his possessions. He loved his things, and they gave him real pleasure. But in his later years he did talk a lot about what they were worth and how much they'd add to his estate and how they should be divided up. I found these conversations very uncomfortable and the thought of having to fit my life style around his possessions and take care of them a real nightmare. Maybe that's why I took so few of them when he died. Indeed, possessions could be a heavy subject for discussion, but for Maria's sake I had to find a way to give her the right perspective on them. But first, I wanted to make sure that she realized how much her parents had influenced her attitude. My next words confronted her with this reality.

"Maria, I know how you feel. My father had his share of struggles with his possessions, and I think his attitude made me leery of having too many of them. However, you had a much harder time of it with your parents, and I think that's the reason you turned away from money and possessions."

"I'm sure they had a negative effect on me," Maria remarked.

"I find that many people rebel against their parents' pre-

occupation with this subject, but in doing so they sometimes go to the other extreme and give up more than they
should. I know a man who was so angry at his mother's at-
tempts to control him that he tried to give her back a $2
million trust she had set up for him. He was damaged by
drugs and alcohol and had no means of support other than
the trust. I persuaded him not to and got the mother to give
him the trust outright."

"You did him a good service," Maria acknowledged.

"I'm not so sure. The man is still in rebellion and is spending the money as fast as he can. He was so angered by his
family's attitude toward money and possessions that he
can't find any value in either. I've tried my best to help him
change his attitude, but haven't succeeded." I paused for a
moment and then continued. "Until he learns to value himself, I don't think he'll ever value his possessions."

"Why do you say that?" Maria asked.

"Because I'm convinced that our possessions are merely
reflections of who we are, and in this case the man has such
a low estimation of himself that he is unable to value his
possessions."

"I never thought of making that connection," Maria said.

"I didn't either until I worked as a consultant. In helping
people with their finances, I discovered that those who
knew who they were valued what they had, but those who
didn't couldn't, because they didn't know what they really
needed."

Maria caught on. "They bought things just for the sake of
buying," she said.

"Yes, and for false reasons, like 'keeping up with the
Joneses' or making themselves feel more important. You
know the type. They have to have all the latest gadgets, most
of which they don't use."

"I know. But my parents aren't like that. I think they like
the security of having things."

"That's another common reason. People think having

possessions and money will automatically give them security. It doesn't. In fact, these things usually add to people's stress since there is always the fear of losing them or having them break down."

"That's true. I remember my parents were always afraid of having things stolen. They spent a lot of money on an alarm system."

"Many people do. The sad thing is that all of our concern about possessions often turns us off from trying to be prosperous."

"It turned me off," Maria said with conviction.

"It did me also, until I started reading *Emmanuel's Book* by Pat Rodegast."[11]

"Who is Emmanuel?" Maria asked.

"He's a so-called spiritual entity channeled by Pat Rodegast."

"That's interesting."

"I don't know how it works, but I find Emmanuel's thoughts compelling. You might want to read his book." I paused to see Maria's reaction. She looked interested, so I continued. "Emmanuel gave me a different understanding of what material prosperity meant."

"What did he say?"

"He asks us to see money and material things as 'materialized consciousness.' He recognized that we need food and clothing and a beautiful home to live in. He calls these things 'accoutrements of self-love.' In acknowledging our self-love, we can't deny ourselves money and our material life. He says that 'self-love will open our hands to receive as well as give.' "

"I like that," Maria affirmed.

"So do I. Emmanuel also calls the universe 'boundless' and says that if we could learn how to receive, we wouldn't have to struggle to get what we need. He states that we need to release our guilt about money and accept it as part of the Divine Universe. To him prosperity is a divine right."

"I never thought of it that way."

"It was a revelation to me. Thinking about it in terms of self-love convinced me to want it. But in working with clients, I learned that just accumulating money and possessions for one's self doesn't make one prosperous in Emmanuel's terms. I see too many selfish, wealthy people who still feel a lack. To be truly prosperous I think people have to have a spiritual appreciation for their wealth. Without that their property has little meaning and often becomes a burden instead of a joy."

"What do you mean by 'a spiritual appreciation'?" Maria asked.

"I mean an appreciation other than selfish greed." I stopped and searched for the right words. "I guess what I mean is that their wealth must be a meaningful adjunct to their life. For example: a man buys a painting because he thinks it's a bargain. His sole interest is in making money. The painting doesn't enrich his life. It's just another profit trophy for his ego. It doesn't make the man prosperous.

"Another man buys a painting because he loves it. *That* painting helps to make the man prosperous."

"Do you think a dishwasher could make one prosperous? I don't love dishwashers." There was a twinkle in Maria's eyes as she asked this question.

"Yes. Because the machine helps us. It relieves us of having to wash the dishes," I said, laughingly. "I think there are lots of practical possessions which in their usefulness can be appreciated since they free us up to do really meaningful things."

"Okay," Maria conceded.

I went on. "And you don't have to have a lot to be prosperous. I know a woman who lives on a social security payment of $251 per month who is prosperous. She feels she has all she needs and that she is rich with the possessions she owns."

"It's really a state of mind, isn't it?" Maria asked.

"Yes," I replied. "But prosperity is more than a state of mind. It's also a state of meeting material needs with a sense of fulfillment."

Maria became thoughtful. I decided it was time to bring her back to the practical world of finances.

"What do you think is the value of the possessions you own now?" I asked.

"I don't know. It's not much."

"Do you think they're worth $2,000?"

"Maybe. If you include my furniture."

"Do you feel prosperous?" I asked, laughingly.

"No, I can't say I am," Maria joined in my laughter. "I need some clothes and books and other things. But I don't have the money to buy them."

"Maybe Emmanuel's philosophy will give you the incentive to allow yourself to earn the money you need."

"I think I'm getting there," Maria said with a smile, and our session ended there.

*   *   *

Maria's case was different from most of my clients in that she was turned off from having possessions. Normally I'm trying to help people cope with the possessions they have or want to buy.

TRISH

In an unusual case I consulted with a woman named Trish who couldn't afford to live with her past. In looking at Trish's financial picture I saw that she was living beyond her means because she was spending too much on a second home. I asked her why she kept the home. She said that she had inherited a historic house from her parents and couldn't bring herself to part with it. She had even preserved all the furniture and the grounds. I asked Trish if she spent much time there. She said she didn't. She and her family went there twice a year. I wondered why the place had such a hold on her, and she confessed that she had spent many happy growing-up years there. I suggested that she was trying to preserve a past life, and she agreed. In recent years her husband had divorced her, and she was searching for remnants of happiness, hoping she could find them in restoring the home and her memories in it.

I advised Trish that she couldn't live over her youth and that the place was exhausting her of her own resources. Psychologically and financially she was being trapped by her family possessions. To emphasize my point, I reminded her that her income and expense projection for the next year showed an estimated overspending of $25,000. Even though she was a wealthy woman, she couldn't afford this kind of deficit.

Though Trish admitted that what I said was true, she was reluctant to sell the place. However, she said that she would think it over. Several months later I spoke with her. She had sold most of her furniture in the home, but still hadn't the heart to put the place on the market. I said nothing, but felt sad for this woman who couldn't let go of her past.

Too often we hang on to possessions that serve our memories but not ourselves. The shirt we once loved but now doesn't fit, the jewelry we were given from parents that we'll never wear, the picture in the closet we inherited from Dad. These items don't inspire us. They merely keep us captive. If we could detach ourselves from these items and clean them out, we could make more room for our spiritual needs. Every year we need to get rid of the stuff we don't need and focus our purchases on the essential items we do need.

But realizing how our money attitudes often block us from doing this, I make sure that people are aware of their attitudes so that they can deal with them. Often these attitudes show up when they are discussing their family money backgrounds.

STEWART

A student named Stewart traced his money hang-ups to his father, a fundamentalist Baptist minister who was poor all his life. His father was terrified of taking responsibility for anything, especially his family, and he rationalized that if he didn't have money, he didn't have an obligation to support his children. He even used his religion as a cop-out.

As Stewart goes on to say in his report, his father was so afraid that he was even able to find a religious discipline which not only sanctioned his financial outlook, but encouraged it. He chose a Judeo-Christian tradition which said that money was evil and should be shunned.

Although Stewart knew that his father's attitude was contrived out of his own fears and shouldn't be listened to, he still had a voice in his head that said it was not okay to have money and possessions and to live comfortably.

Fortunately as he was writing this report, he heard another voice saying that the universe is a celebration of bounty and abundance and that it is his purpose to flourish to the best of his ability.

During our classes together, we wrestled with both of these voices, and Stewart found his voice in a balanced attitude which realized the negatives of having too many possessions and the positives of having meaningful possessions. For him, as with all of us, it was a matter of creating the right balance.

Yet most of us at times get so absorbed in our material desires that we not only can't balance our money and possessions, but also can't see them in a spiritual light.

Now I'll share with you a report from a student who through great deprivation learned the meaning of this materialism.

JAY'S REPORT

"I grew up in a small suburban town. My parents

divorced when I was young, and my eight brothers and sisters grew up with my mother, who was ill throughout my childhood. Money seemed always to be a major worry. There never seemed enough for the mortgage payment, the phone bill, the utilities, new shoes, let alone any of the things my peers had or that were advertised on TV.

"This concept of 'not enough' has remained with me, coloring my perceptions and preventing me from hoping too much. I went to work at age thirteen in a factory and have worked ever since. I know that I can survive. That I can get by with very little, if need be. I have gone without food and water, shelter, automobiles, and new clothes.

"My attitudes toward money have kept me from consuming too much and have forced me to keep my needs simple. Yet I also realize that I suspect and fear having money. 'Money is the root of all evil' is an underlying script which runs through my mind at times.

"Now I feel the crunch of not having enough and my need to achieve my goal of helping others and live in balance on the earth. I don't want to accumulate a lot of things, but I do want to learn and acquire tools (of therapy) to help others. I also would like leisure time to appreciate the wonder and beauty of life."

It's rare that I can find someone like Jay who has suffered greatly from want, but still has an ideal purpose for owning money and possessions. To me Jay's report is a powerful testimony on how one can keep a nonmaterial vision in life through all the material hardships one may face.

I have worked with others who have had similar backgrounds, and most of them let their fears dominate their money thinking. To make up for their own deprivation they try to accumulate as many possessions and as much money as they can. In the process they usually lose friends, health, and the joy of living.

Leila and I had a particularly painful experience when a good friend of ours named Taylor rejected our friendship because we didn't choose him to act as our agent when we sold our house. We called him up and tried to explain that we had chosen another agent because she had gotten us our current home and been instrumental in introducing us to the community. Taylor wouldn't listen to us, and I realized that he felt we had betrayed him.

In reasoning out his attitude, I concluded that it stemmed from his poverty background. In his early years Taylor had lived off of charity, and, because of his previous lack, money was so important to him that for us not to let him have the opportunity to have the commission on the sale of our house was an unpardonable breach of conduct. Loss of money for him equaled a loss of friendship. How sad, but understandable in his mind-set.

Normally in helping people assess their possessions, I don't get a chance to delve into their family money, but have to focus on the immediate, practical issues.

With many families control is a major issue, and I see it most dramatically when couples are in the midst of a divorce and have to divide up their properties.

LAUREN

Recently a woman named Lauren came to me for an objective opinion on the fairness of her husband's proposed out-of-court divorce settlement. Her husband was an astute businessman who managed his own company, which was jointly owned in his and Lauren's name. Lauren was employed as a vice president, though she had little knowledge of the company and did only routine jobs for her husband. The couple also jointly owned a rental property and a residence.

Lauren's husband's lawyer had drawn up the divorce papers, and they stipulated that Lauren would get the rental property, and her husband would get the company and the residency. In addition the company would retain Lauren as an employee and pay her $100,000 ($20,000 per year for five years).

Lauren was upset because her husband wouldn't let her look at the company's books, and she knew her share of the company was worth a lot more than $100,000. As evidence she cited her tax return, which showed that she was paid $120,000 in wages last year.

In our discussion of these details Lauren explained that she wasn't so concerned about getting a fair share of the company, but she hated the way her husband tried to control her. It was just like him to dictate terms without giving her information. Moreover, during their marriage, she had given up her sculpture work to help him with his company, and now she resented having done that.

I advised her that she shouldn't accept his terms. Under the state's laws, she was entitled to half of their communal properties, and she could press for an equal share of the company and other assets. I also thought that it was wrong for her to stay on the company payroll, since by doing so she would remain under his thumb. I explained that he was suggesting this only so that he could write off his payments to her as a business expense through his company and thereby reduce his taxes, but it still made her his employee.

She didn't like that idea either. In fact, it was totally against what she was trying to do—namely, to break away from him so that she could reassert herself. She confessed that she had lost a lot of her self-esteem in this relationship which she needed to get back.

I told her it was very important for her to feel equal to him, and it was worth going to court if she had to.

She suggested that I meet with her and her lawyer and go over the terms of the divorce. I agreed, and in the following week we had our meeting.

Before our second session, Lauren had thought about what she wanted and decided that she wouldn't accept staying as an employee for the company, but would agree to the payment. She didn't think it was worth going to court over the company. He had the company before she married him, and he would fight to the end to keep it. I said that was fine, if it didn't undermine her self-esteem to accept less than half its value. She said it didn't. Being on the company payroll was her big concern.

We worked out that she should ask for either a lump sum payment or alimony. The payment would not be taxable to her since it would be considered as part of a division of property. The alimony, however, would be taxable, and she should ask for a larger amount to cover the income taxes she would have to pay. She agreed, so we increased the annual payment from $20,000 to $25,000 for the five years. That meant she would receive $125,000 instead of the $100,000, if he chose to pay her in alimony.

Since she really wanted the rental building, she was willing to receive that and along with its mortgage in exchange for his getting their residence. I asked if she felt comfortable assuming the mortgage on the rental property. She said she was since the rents more than covered the mortgage payments, and if she used it as her primary residence she could live there rent free.

Once we got the major property items resolved, we had no difficulty dividing up the joint checking accounts, savings, debts, and other items. On taxes, Lauren was adamant that her husband pay for any legal or accounting fees incurred. She said that he had always done the taxes, and she knew nothing about them; so if the IRS questioned them, he was responsible for the costs of defending their position.

As we went through the legal document, I was fascinated to watch the change in Lauren. She became stronger with each decision she made, and when we finished she was definitely in control of the situation. All the uncertainty she had when she first talked with me was gone. I could see how this process of dividing possessions had been an important step in her liberation. In defining her divorce terms she had taken back her power.

Aside from supervising the division of possessions, I'm often asked to help people determine when they should liquidate them.

To determine this, I compare the total amount of money they have in cash, checking accounts, and savings with the total amount they have in their home, car, and other properties and possessions. If I find that they have too little in the former and an excess in the latter, I suggest that they sell some of their possessions to get a little more ready money. In these times most of us need readily available funds for emergencies.

BARRY

A case in point occurred several years ago when a young man named Barry came to me and said that he was desperate to have some money because his mother back east had just been taken to the hospital and he needed money to purchase an airplane ticket. His credit card was maxed out, and he knew no one in town who could lend him money.

I had him write down a list of everything he owned and found nothing that he could sell. I had all but given up when Barry reached into his pocket to get his wallet and out dropped his car keys. As he stooped to pick them up, I noticed a safe-deposit box key was attached to his key ring.

I asked Barry if he had a safe-deposit box. He said he did, but there wasn't anything in it except some old insurance papers his father had left him. I suggested we take a look at them to see if they had any value.

He went to the box and returned with them the next day. I looked them over and discovered that his father had left

Barry a paid-up insurance policy which was worth $2,000. After his father died, Barry had put it in the box without looking at it.

I told Barry that he could turn in the policy and get the funds. This was more than Barry needed to make his journey.

Barry's case reminds us of the importance of knowing the value of what we have, since it is all a part of knowing who we are. Yet we can't let possessions possess our souls, so in taking stock of ourselves we need to assess our true feelings about them to make sure they are the right ones for us.

*   *   *

Exercises:

1. Make a rough estimate of the value of your possessions and properties, excluding your car and home.

2. Review your possessions and try to see how they reflect who you are. Note that as you change, your possessions will change.

3. Sort out the possessions you don't need and get rid of them.

4. Before purchasing an item, meditate on whether or not it is the right one for you. If you have any doubts, hold off on your purchase.

5. Total your cash, checking accounts, and savings. Compare this total to the total value of your possessions. If you think you need more available funds, sell some of your possessions.

10

Meeting Your Commitments

Debts and Credit

"SIGN ON the dotted line," were the words my friend heard in the background over the phone as he was starting to talk to his son.

"I'm having a chair built for $1,600," his son said. "I'm in the store now."

"That's great," the father said, though he wasn't sure how his son could afford to spend so much on a chair.

"The guy is willing to give me credit," his son explained. "He says he'll let me pay for it over the next six months."

"Good," his father said. Now he understood the voice he had heard in the background. It was the storekeeper asking his son to sign the credit agreement.

"I know I can handle it," his son said.

"I'm sure you can," his father replied, and their conversation ended there.

My friend had shared this telephone call with me in response to my asking him how his son was coping with AIDS. My friend thought that his son's purchase of a chair was a hopeful sign since it indicated that he was expecting to live long enough to pay for it.

"It's another act of defiance against his disease," my friend said.

For me the son's purchase was a good example of how one's debt can be tied to one's spirit. In this case the son was using his credit to bolster his immune system!

I never considered the psychological effects that bills and debts could have on me until I left the brokerage business and became an investment advisor. With my income cut in half, I found myself struggling to meet my expenses. Under this stress I became overly judgmental of how we were spending our money and how much people were charging us. Though I never became seriously depressed, I felt a lot of anxiety.

In my quest for peace of mind, I tried a simple visualization exercise to relieve me of the tension I felt when I was getting ready to pay my bills. Just before I started to write checks, I would close my eyes and surround myself with an imaginary white light. I would visualize this light flowing through every part of my body. As I felt the light move down through my head, shoulders, chest, and feet, I could feel the tension leave me. When I was completely relaxed, I'd open my eyes and write the checks. This exercise calmed my nerves and helped me overcome my resistance to paying bills.

Several months later, I picked up a book called *Creating Money* by Sanaya Roman and Duane Packer that was recommended by one of my friends. In leafing through its pages, I came upon a passage which spoke directly to me. It started, "When you don't know where your money will come from to pay your bills . . . you may be dealing with fear."[12] It went on to say that to release your fear you need to identify what you are afraid of by asking the question, "What is the worst that can happen to me if I don't pay my bills this month?"

I thought over this question and decided it was a good one to ask myself in my next meditation. When I asked it, the answer I got wasn't what I expected. I assumed my fear would be about having no money, starving, not being able to support my family, having to beg or borrow to live, or having to look for a higher paying job. Instead my fear had to do with my self-image. I feared that if I didn't have money to pay my bills, I'd lose my self-respect.

Recognizing this fear and its implications helped to reduce my anxiety, it forced me to remember that my worth was measured by who I was as a person not by how much money I had. Therefore, my self-esteem couldn't be depleted by my lack of funds.

Impressed with this exercise, I read through Roman and Packer's book. In it I found many other helpful suggestions for changing my attitude. The most important message I got was that "Fears lose their power when you hold them up to the light of your consciousness."[13] I had to confront my anxieties about my bills before I could change my feeling toward them.

Slowly my attitude improved, but I still overly criticized myself and others for bills that I felt were inappropriate or wrong. I had read that for centuries people in the East used mantras to successfully control their minds. Since affirmations are similar to mantras, I decided to try repeating an affirmation to put a rein on my thinking about the injustice of my bills.

I usually memorized one of Catherine Ponder's affirmations from her book, *The Healing Secrets of the Ages*.[14] I'd repeat the affirmation silently every time I found myself judging a bill. I found that doing this stopped my negative thinking, and, if I repeated the affirmation long enough, the words discharged my angry feelings.

While I was trying to change my mind-set, I took concrete steps to appreciate my bills and take better control of them. Before I paid any bill, I took a moment to recognize the goods or services I had received. Be it the telephone, the electricity, the trash pickup, or the plumber, I gave them a silent "thank you" and wrote "thank you" on the checks I sent out.

When bills came in, I immediately scanned them to see if there were any problems which we had to address. I set up a routine whereby I paid the monthly bills on the first of the month, and other bills within a few days of their arrival.

Confronting these obligations took a lot of the anxiety out of them, and paying them on a regular basis made it easier for me to see how well we were living within our monthly income. If toward the end of the month there wasn't enough money to cover our expenses, we would put off bills to the following month or simply reduce our spending. This moment-to-moment monitoring dissolved our greatest fear— that of not knowing where we stood.

Having myself struggled with these obligations, I could empathize with clients who were similarly overwhelmed with their bills, and I shared with them my approach. With those who had long-term debts, mortgages, credit card balances, car loans, etc., I had them make up a list of these obligations, showing the type of loan, the monthly payment, the outstanding balance, and the interest rate.

After making this list, we'd look at their debts in the context of their total financial picture. If we thought they were too high, I would show them how they could reduce them or make them easier to manage. This could include paying off, consolidating, refinancing, or extending loans.

Once I thought people understood their debts and felt

secure enough to deal with them, I would discuss the effects of these debts on their emotions. Most people were searching for the same peace of mind I was and would do what was necessary to attain it even if it cost them money. Sometimes if I thought the stress of having debts was not as great as the stress of trying to pay them off, I'd advise people to keep them.

In rare cases where I found people's loans were so overwhelming that they were creating a serious depression, I would suggest that they consider going into bankruptcy. While most people initially balked at doing this, when they understood that it didn't necessarily mean they would have to lose their home, car, and personal possessions, or their self-identity, they were willing to open their minds to it. For many, being able to reorganize or release debts was a healing process and one that brought immediate relief from their distress.

Different loans pose different problems. The most difficult ones are the family loans since they are usually part of a whole complex of familial emotional issues.

This was what I felt Maria might be up against when in our ninth session she told me that she was thinking of asking her father for a loan.

MARIA'S NINTH SESSION

Maria seemed more preoccupied than usual as we started the session.

"Is anything bothering you, Maria?" I asked.

"I'm concerned about my tuition bill," she replied.

"What's the matter?"

"I don't have enough money to cover this semester."

"What will you do?"

"I'm thinking of asking my dad for a loan."

"Okay."

"But I really don't want to."

"I know. You don't want to be under his control."

"Yes. And I'm afraid he won't give it to me."

"He still might. You can't tell. But I think you should be businesslike about asking for it. Borrowing in families can be sticky."

"It scares me."

"Have you borrowed money before?" I asked.

"A few small loans from friends," Maria replied.

"Do you have any loans now?"

"No."

"Well, I was going to discuss debts today anyhow, so we can talk about your father's loan once you have some understanding of how loans work." I paused a moment while Maria shifted in her chair. Then I continued.

"Borrowing money (I don't mean getting credit cards) has become a lot more complicated than it used to be. When I was growing up there weren't many loans available, and they required much less documentation. Lenders were more concerned about the character of the individual than they were about his or her assets and liabilities. Now a person's financial picture is the principal character reference lenders want."

Maria grimaced. "That doesn't sound good."

"It isn't. I had a friend tell me that when he first came to town in 1970, he had no job and had just enough money for a month's rent. He found work, but had no established credit, so Sears wouldn't let him buy a refrigerator. He went to the local bank, talked with a bank officer, and she lent him the money for the refrigerator on a handshake. Now he has a thriving business, more than twenty years of good credit, and when he last went to borrow money at the same bank, they asked for his personal and business statements, credit references, a credit report, and that he keep a minimum balance in his checking account."

"All that!" Maria exclaimed.

"Doesn't show much trust, does it?"

"No."

"Yet trust is an essential part of any successful loan." I paused and then added, "I think a loan is as much a spiritual commitment as it is a financial one."

"I never thought of it that way, but I see it is."

"It's a commitment one has to live up to, and it takes will power as well as money," I said.

"I guess it does," Maria mused.

"To borrow from your father, you'll want to create a mutual trust between the two of you."

"How can I do that?" Maria asked.

"By being as businesslike as you can," I replied. "I think you'll need to show him your financial picture."

"I will?" Maria looked incredulous.

"Yes. From what you've told me, your father is very concerned about money, and you'll have to be very open about your financial situation to get his trust."

"You're probably right." I caught a note of resignation in Maria's voice, but disregarded it.

"And you'll have to spell out the terms of the loan."

"Will you help me?" Maria asked.

"Yes," I replied, "but before we go any further I want to give you some basic loan information. You'll need this knowledge to earn your father's respect and convince him you know what you are doing."

"Which I don't," Maria said forlornly.

"But you will," I said laughingly. "Let's begin with some basic lending terms. There are five terms you need to know to deal with most any loan: *principal, principal payments, interest, interest payments,* and the *balance outstanding.*" I wrote the terms down on a notepad I had in front of me and showed them to Maria. I then began to explain them in the order that I wrote them down.

"*Principal* is the amount of the loan itself. If you need $5,000 from your father, the principal of the loan is $5,000."

Maria nodded so I continued on to the next term. "The

principal payments are the dollar payments you make to repay the loan. With most loans you repay them over a period of time. Say one to five years. However, there are some loans in which the total amount is repaid at the end of a specified time. It might be a year. Do you follow me?"

"Yes."

I moved to the next term on the list—*interest.* "*Interest* is the percentage of the principal you pay as a fee for borrowing the money. In the case with your father you might suggest a charge of 8%, which would be a little below what banks are now charging individuals for personal loans."

"Is the charge always made as a percentage?" Maria questioned.

"Yes."

I continued down the list. "Now *interest payments* are the dollar payments you make to repay the interest."

"Are the interest and principal payments made separately?" Maria asked.

"Normally you combine the amounts into one payment. But it's important to keep separate accounting records for them."

"Why?"

"Because interest can be calculated differently for different loans and the schedules of interest and principal payments can vary. Also there can be different tax consequences in paying principal and in paying interest. For example, you can deduct interest payments off your income taxes on the mortgage of your home, but you can't deduct principal payments."

"Sounds complicated," Maria said.

"It can be," I replied. "But under the law a lender has to show you in writing the costs of your loan and the different payments so that you don't have to do the calculating."

"That's good," Maria said.

"And to find out the tax consequences," I continued, "you only have to ask an accountant." I paused for a moment to think about how Maria would handle the loan with her father.

"In your case you could work out the terms of the loan with your father and then get a bank to give you a schedule payment that fits what you both want."

"That sounds easy enough," Maria sounded relieved.

I glanced down on the sheet of paper to the last term I had written—*balance outstanding.* I went on.

"Now the *balance outstanding* refers to the amount of principal and/or interest that has not been paid back. Lenders and borrowers both need to keep these balances to know how much is owed." I smiled at Maria. "You'll have to keep a record of your payments to your father," I said.

"Okay," she replied.

We sat in silence, as Maria looked again at the terms on the list.

"Do these terms seem clear?" I asked.

"Yes, I think I understand them," Maria replied.

"Then let's look at the major types of loans you can get." I took another page from my pad and wrote down a list of loans. Again I showed the list to Maria.

"The principal ones are *mortgages, secured loans, credit card loans, installment loans,* and *personal loans.*" I paused as Maria read the list.

"Let's go over them," I said.

"Okay," Maria replied.

"*Mortgages* are long-term loans used for buying homes and buildings, so they wouldn't be applicable to your dad's loan." Maria nodded, so I continued to the next loan.

"A *secured loan* is a loan that is backed by something of value like an investment, and since you don't have anything you can put up for security, your father wouldn't offer you a secured loan. Does that make sense?"

"Yes."

I stopped before going on to *credit card loans.* Although I knew that Maria wouldn't be able to get a credit card loan from her dad, I wanted to find out how much she knew about these loans. So instead of defining the loan, I began asking Maria questions about her own cards.

"Maria, do you have a credit card?" I asked.

"Yes," she replied. "A MasterCard. But I haven't used it much."

"Do you have an instant card?"

"Yes. I use that one quite often."

"Do you know the difference between these cards?" I asked.

"I think so," Maria replied hesitantly. "The credit card company sends me a bill each month. When I use the instant card, the money is immediately taken out of my account."

"Good. I'm glad you recognize the difference. Which card is harder to manage?"

"The instant card," Maria answered promptly. "I have trouble keeping track of it."

"All debit cards—that is, cards which make direct charges to your account—are tough to handle. I know one woman who had a debit VISA card through a brokerage house and couldn't stop using it. Finally she put it in water and froze it in her freezer. It stopped her, but I'm not sure the card will be usable," I smiled.

"She was pretty extreme," Maria laughed.

"The point is these cards can be dangerous, and I wouldn't use them except in emergencies."

"What about my regular VISA card?" Maria asked.

"I would use it as I would a charge account—that is, pay it off every month."

"What if you can't afford to?" Maria asked.

"I wouldn't make the purchase with the card if I couldn't," I replied.

"I see."

"I remember when my kids were abroad, we'd get enormous telephone bills on our charge cards. I was always tempted to pay the minimum amount. It seemed so insignificant compared to the total."

"I would," Maria said.

"But then I thought about the interest I would have to pay and the large balances that would be outstanding which sooner or later I'd have to face, and I'd write the check for the whole amount." I sighed.

"I bet that upset you," Maria said with a twinkle in her eye.

"It did, but I accepted it as my karma." We laughed.

After a brief silence, I returned to Maria's loan problem. "I don't think your father would want to give you a credit card loan," I said with a smile.

Maria laughed again and shook her head no.

"So going back to our list of loans, that leaves us with the possibility of an *installment loan* or a *personal loan*."

"Okay."

"With the *installment loan* you usually have to repay your loan in monthly installments. Let's say you agreed to have an installment loan from your father for $5,000 at 8% interest for five years. You would have to repay the loan in monthly amounts over the five years."

"I guess I could do that."

"You could, but you might want to have the flexibility of paying it off when you want to."

"That would be good."

"Since the *personal loan* permits you to do that, it might be your best bet."

"How does it work?" Maria asked.

"A *personal loan* is a very flexible loan," I replied. "It is a multipurposed, nonsecured loan which you can pay back in a lump sum or in installments."

"That sounds best. So I'll ask Dad for a personal loan."

"I would. And if I were you, I'd ask him if he would let you pay him back when you are earning enough money to support yourself."

"I like that idea, too," Maria said.

"But you should offer to pay him interest on the loan so that he sees it as a business deal."

"Okay. How much should I borrow?"

"That will depend on what your financial picture looks like. We'll have to look at your income and expenses to determine that."

"Can we do that now?" Maria asked.

"I'd like to wait until we've had a few more sessions," I replied, "and you've got a real understanding of your other finances." I paused and then asked, "Can you last that long?"

"I think I can. I should have enough money for the next two months."

"I think borrowing from your father won't be easy since he is critical of what you're doing. I want you to be fully prepared before you ask."

"Okay."

"I know that asking for this money will be hard for you. I want to be sure we do it right."

"So do I," Maria replied, as our session ended.

*   *   *

My desire to prepare Maria fully before she asked her father for a loan stemmed from my knowledge of the difficulties inherent in loans from one family member to another. The anxieties and frustration these commitments engendered in parents were often passed down to their children.

A good example of how this happens was written in the report from a student named Louise who was upset by a loan that her father took out.

LOUISE'S REPORT

"My mother and father never had a strong, loving relationship as far as I can remember. They relied on my three brothers and myself for the emotional and psychological support they couldn't get from each other. Their dysfunction fed into our financial situation, as their personal frustrations with each other were converted into joint anger over the family's money difficulties.

"My father didn't confide in my mother, and I remember my mother on numerous occasions feeling betrayed and ripping up the checkbook and credit cards. Once I found her sitting in a corner sobbing. She had just found out that my father had forged her name to take out a loan. I could feel the shame and humiliation she felt. The lack of money in my family was a scarlet letter burned into my psyche."

When loans are presented under such negative circumstances, they can't help but engender anxiety. Fortunately, Louise could see that the "forged" loan was merely a symbol of her parents' "forged" relationship and that she didn't have to be caught up in their emotions. During the course she was able to disassociate herself from her mother's anxiety and frustration, and this helped to give her the courage to manage her own debts.

Louise's case also points out what I have said before about the connection between money and spirit. The spirit is the guiding force in money matters, and its problems create the money concerns. Thus, whenever we have financial worries we need to examine not only the facts but the feelings behind them.

JERRY'S CASE

I had another good illustration of this connection when a twenty-three-year-old man named Jerry complained that he had a terrible credit rating. He hadn't realized it until he had tried to get a Sears credit card. Sears had turned him down on the basis of his poor rating at the credit bureau.

I suggested that he have the credit bureau send him his report. Jerry did, and he discovered that he had a $2 American Express debt outstanding since 1987 and a $465 hospital bill that was two years old. We both thought it odd that American Express would put a lien for $2 but it had. It was a holdover from a travel bill that Jerry couldn't identify. The hospital bill referred to an operation Jerry had had in 1989.

I asked Jerry why he wasn't aware of these debts. He said that his mother required him to send all bills to her. Her secretary paid them, and he never kept track of them. Sometimes the bills were sent directly to his mother, and he never saw them. His mother also gave him $500 a month for miscellaneous living expenses.

Jerry thought that both bills on his credit report were ones that had been sent directly to his mother and that he had never seen them.

He had gone to college and was now training to be an actor. Until recently he had worked at several part-time jobs, but they didn't pay enough so he still depended on his mother.

I told Jerry that it was time for him to take control of his own finances. He agreed, but confessed he had no idea how to do it. His mother had never let him, and he had developed a fear of handling money. He could hardly write a check, much less balance his checkbook. He never knew how much money he had or where it went.

I asked Jerry how good his relationship was with his mother. He said it was difficult. His mother wouldn't listen to him and didn't like the fact that he wanted to be an actor, since she believed there was little money to be made in the theater. She was also afraid that Jerry wouldn't be able to cope for himself.

I told Jerry that I thought there was a real issue of control with his mother and that he needed to break away from her for his own psychological health. I suggested that we draw up a summary of his finances and calculate how much he needed for his monthly living expenses. Then Jerry would ask his mother for that amount and pay his own bills. I could help him if he needed it.

Jerry liked my idea, but wasn't sure his mother would go for it. I suggested that he write his mother and tell her the details of my proposal, explaining that at twenty-three he was an adult and it was time for him to be on his own.

Jerry sent the letter, but had no reply. When he called his mother, she put him off saying that she was in such a rush she couldn't talk about it. Jerry didn't think she had actually read the letter.

In our next session we discussed what this meant and agreed that his mother didn't want to give up her control and wasn't willing to face the issue. We realized that, for her, money and love were closely tied together and that through the control of Jerry's purse strings she hoped to manipulate his love.

We agreed that the only thing to do was to send the money request directly to his mother's secretary and hope that she would send the funds. At other times the secretary had sent the money without talking to his mother.

This time, however, when Jerry called in his request, the secretary put him through to his mother, and she got very angry at him for wanting so much money. Jerry reminded her of the letter he wrote, and she backed off in confusion. Jerry held his position, and finally his mother agreed to send the money, but she wanted a complete accounting for it with copies of the bills. Jerry talked to me about this accounting, and we agreed he should do it. Getting his freedom was worth it.

It still took Jerry several more calls before his mother sent the money. Each time he called, she would start the conversation, "I'm sending it. I'm sending it." But no money would come. Finally, and only after Jerry pleaded for the money so that he could pay for his car repairs and get it out of the mechanic's shop, did his mother relent.

In this case I had the credit bureau to thank for helping me discover Jerry's money problem. If I hadn't asked Jerry to find out about his poor credit, I might never have realized that the source of the problem was not Jerry, but his mother!

Besides helping us deal with psychological problems like the one I encountered with Jerry, our debts can bring people closer together.

GORDON AND LISA

A case in point was Gordon and Lisa. Their marriage was undergoing stress because of their debts, and they sought my advice on what to do.

I helped them draw up their financial summary, and when we looked at it, we found that it showed they had a total of about $12,000 in investments in Individual Retirement Accounts, $17,000 in car and credit card loans, and they were overspending by about $300 per month.

We went over their expenses and, as we expected, the largest costs besides their mortgage payment were the payments on their car loans and credit cards which totaled more than $800 per month.

They both admitted having credit cards was a real strain on their marriage, as they often argued about what to do with them. Gordon wanted to have only one card that they could both use, but Lisa wanted to keep the cards she had in her name so that she could maintain her credit.

Gordon thought he ought to get another job and earn the money to pay off these loans, but Lisa didn't want him to. She felt that he would spend less time with the family, and she resented his being away so much as it was.

I suggested that they retain their cards, but pay down their loan balances even though it would cost them a penalty tax to take money from their IRAs.

I told them I normally didn't suggest doing this, but because they were overspending by $300 per month and their monthly loan payments were more than they could manage, they would be better off reducing their loans and their payments. I pointed out that they were earning only 8% on the investments in the IRA and were paying 14% interest on their credit cards.

At first the couple balked at doing this. When I said that I was more concerned about their marriage than their having money for retirement or the extra costs they would have to pay, they agreed to take $7,000 from their IRAs to pay off their most expensive loans.

I also asked them not to charge additional amounts on their cards until they had paid off their balances. After that, they should use the cards as charge cards, which meant that they had to be paid off every month.

Neither was sure he or she would be able to stop using the cards since both had gotten so dependent on them. I suggested that they seal their cards in an envelope and put them in their safe-deposit box until they were paid off. The couple thought this was a good idea.

We went over their car loans and discovered that the loan balance on their Chevrolet was more than its market value. Since the Chevrolet was giving them trouble, they decided that as soon as they got any extra money, they would pay down that loan so that they would be in a better position to sell the car, if necessary.

We then examined their other monthly expenses to see if there was any way Gordon and Lisa could reduce these costs. They found that if they cut back on their dining-out and baby-sitting expenses, they could save more than $150 per month. Gordon volunteered to do more baby-sitting when Lisa had evening engagements.

When the couple left, I was struck by how much closer they seemed than when they came in. Figuring out how to manage their loan commitments had forced Gordon and Lisa to come together, and I felt certain that their marriage would survive their credit cards.

If we are willing to show the same responsibility for our debts as Gorden and Lisa showed with theirs, we will have peace of mind knowing that we have met our commitments.

*   *   *

Exercises for Changing Attitude Toward Bills and Debts:

1. Just before paying your bills, visualize yourself surrounded by white light. Stay with this light until you are completely relaxed. Then begin paying your bills.

2. Identify the fears you have by asking yourself in meditation: "What is the worst thing that can happen if I don't pay my bills this month?" Once you've identified your fear, see the illusion it has created. With this recognition your fear will diminish.

3. When you catch yourself being overly critical of your bills and debts, repeat a positive affirmation until you have let go of your anger.

4. Appreciate the goods and services you receive, thanking the suppliers as you pay their bills.

5. Write "thank you" on the checks you write.

Exercises for Controlling Bills and Debts:

1. Look at your bills and debts as soon as they arrive.

2. Pay your monthly bills routinely at the beginning, middle, or end of the month.

3. Pay other bills within several days of their arrival.

4. Monitor your income and expenses throughout the month to make sure you are living within your budget. If you aren't, reduce your expenses. Try to stay within a monthly income goal.

5. Make a list of debts. Include the type of loan, the balance outstanding, the monthly payment, and the interest rate. Total the monthly payments and the outstanding balance.

6. Draw up a financial summary of money and property, debts and monthly income, and expenses. See summary on page 237.

7. Review the interest rates on your loans. Consider paying off the more expensive loans with any available funds you have on your summary.

8. Consider combining your loans into one loan that is less expensive than the others.

9. Consider refinancing loans which have a high interest rate.

10. Consider extending your loans over a longer period of time to reduce the monthly payment.

If you are considering getting a loan:

I. Draw up a financial summary of your money and properties, debts, and monthly income and expenses (see summary on page 237).

2. Look at your available funds to see if you really need the money.

3. Add your estimated monthly loan payment to your monthly expenses.

4. Compare your monthly income to your monthly expenses, including the monthly loan payment, and see if you can afford the loan.

Before making loans:

1. Meditate on taking the loan. If it doesn't feel right, don't take it.

11

Finding the Right Protection

Insurance

PEOPLE'S FEELINGS of security affect how well they manage their insurance, and those who have money anxieties often can't find the courage to tackle the subject.

I discovered this in my course on "Money and Spirit" when students shared their attitudes toward insurance. Many students, including the wealthier ones, had inherited such a poverty consciousness that they had thought little about owning insurance, much less understanding the intricacies of it.

Warren was such a case, and I share with you his report on his family and money since his attitude was typical of the consciousness I was up against.

WARREN'S REPORT

"My greatest fear of money, believe it or not, comes out of having grown up with lots of it. We lived in a giant, three-story house, yet my mother made us keep the paper towels we used because each sheet cost 25¢ and she thought for that kind of money we'd better be able to use it twice. While she scrimped on paper towels, she thought nothing of having a mink coat and a Mercedes Benz. My father didn't work, and I was raised by a governess who refused to let us bathe regularly or buy new clothes. So for thirteen years I thought all poor people lived in big houses.

"When I was fifteen, I was working to escape my oppressive situation. I paid for everything—clothes, movies, ski trips, etc. I was free and independent, so I thought, until I began to realize that I had become a prisoner of my mother's thinking. I never bought things I needed. I was stingy with my friends, irresponsible with my bills, and I became obsessed with not having enough money."

Warren was one of the most vocal in castigating insurance salespeople and insurance in general. I questioned his attitude and suggested that perhaps it was influenced by his family. He admitted that his parents wouldn't spend an extra penny on insurance and didn't like having to buy it. I asked Warren if they had ever explained to him how their insurance worked; he said they hadn't, and he didn't think they even understood it.

I asked Warren if he knew anything about insurance, and he was frank to admit that the subject overwhelmed him. When he bought his insurance on his car, he hadn't even looked at his policy.

Warren shared this with the class and found that many students felt the same as he did. The majority believed their anxieties stemmed from their parents and their own lack of knowledge.

For Warren and these students this recognition was a major breakthrough in changing their attitude toward insurance. In realizing how prejudiced they were against it, they also realized their need to be open to the benefits of it.

I explained that a major benefit of owning insurance was the psychological security it gave people to know that they had resources to pay for possible accidents and illnesses or damages and losses of property. Several students in the class complained that they couldn't afford to get all the protection they needed, but I assured them that just having some insurance provided a sense of security. I also reminded them that money is energy, and insurance is a form of reserve energy, like investments, which—if used correctly—can be very helpful in creating peace of mind.

Warren said that his father had worried a lot about getting insurance, and it hadn't brought him peace of mind.

I explained to Warren that dealing with insurance could create anxiety if people let their fears dominate their thinking. As an illustration, I shared with the class an experience I had when I tried to get insurance on a rickety, old chicken coop we owned in Maine that the previous tenants had moved into after we bought their property. I had thought that they were going to use the chicken coop only for their pottery business, but they decided to live there, too. The coop had no live-in accommodations, was uninsulated, and had a wood stove and kiln in it. I was concerned about the potential damages that could occur under these circumstances. I tried to persuade them to leave, but they refused.

I knew I needed insurance to protect myself, but I feared that the insurance company wouldn't give it to me if I told them that there were people living in the chicken coop. I remember dreading meeting with the insurance agent.

When I saw him, I couldn't bring myself to tell him about the couple.

The agent was polite, but very quiet as I explained what I wanted. He said he'd be back to me in a few weeks. After I left him, I was mortified at what I had done.

The agent never communicated with me, but I learned later on that he was friends with the couple and knew exactly what they were doing!

This experience forced me to do some soul searching. My fears over getting this insurance had undermined my integrity. At that point in my life I hadn't thought much about incorporating my ideals into my money transactions, and I wasn't strong enough to withstand the temptation to avoid telling the whole truth.

However, the psychological pain I felt was enough to cure me of a second evasive act. I went to another insurance agent and told him the complete story, which included the fears I had about not being able to get insurance, my evading of the truth with the first insurance agent, and the remorse I felt. The agent was sympathetic and said that a lot of people avoid telling the whole story for the same reason I did. He appreciated my honesty and agreed to insure my chicken coop after he had seen it.

I told the class that confronting my insurance fears and dealing with them honestly was a powerful antidote to my guilt and shame.

I don't know if my story motivated Warren to learn about insurance or not, but several weeks later he called because his aunt was moving to Albuquerque, and he wanted my opinion on how she should finance the purchase of her home. As we were reviewing the costs, I mentioned home insurance. To my surprise, he had researched where to get it, how much to buy, and how much it cost. I thought this research was quite a victory for someone who previously was so overwhelmed by his own car insurance that he couldn't look at his policy.

Over the years I've shared with my classes many other anxiety-provoking insurance experiences which undermined my security, but which also forced me to work through my own fears. Most of these experiences had to do with struggling with exorbitant price increases for health and automobile insurance.

However, I had one particularly disillusioning time when our local broker, who represented the insurance company where we had our car insurance, told us that the company was going to discontinue our insurance because of a minor accident we had.

Our insurance was coming up for renewal in less than a month so we were afraid that we wouldn't be able to get coverage before our insurance expired. We scurried around looking for alternative insurance, but found it prohibitively expensive due to the accident we had on our record.

While we were looking, I received another call from our local broker. He told me that there was a chance I could still have my insurance if I switched my home owner's insurance (which wasn't with him) to the automobile company and purchased a combined home-auto policy. Since the company wanted my home insurance business, he thought that they would be willing to continue the insurance on the car despite the accident.

As we were considering the broker's suggestion, we received notice of our annual premium bill from our insurance company. There was no mention about discontinuing our insurance. The insurance cost hadn't even taken into account the accident as the bill was only 10% higher than the previous year—well below the other quotes we got from other insurance companies.

I paid the quarterly installment on the day it arrived, thinking that if the company received the money they couldn't take away my insurance.

Once I was sure my money had been received by the company, I called the local broker and told him that I had received my annual premium notice and paid my first installment. He seemed surprised that the company had sent it and couldn't give me any explanation of what had happened.

I had to conclude that the local broker was trying to frighten me into switching my home insurance to the company which he represented so that he could get more business. I felt betrayed by the broker, but relieved to have my insurance. I promised myself that I would get another broker as soon as possible.

Experiences like this kind depress me, as I see little purpose or meaning in them. When I'm in this state of mind, I find it helpful to turn to thinkers like Thomas Moore. Moore was a monk who for many years lived in solitude until he decided the isolated life was not enough for his soul, so he went into the secular world to find his salvation. In his lectures he talks about the sacredness of all things, and in his book, *Care of the Soul,* he provides a guide for finding soul meaning in our everyday lives. Regarding money, he says that in its power to corrupt us it can be a transformative catalyst. "It (money) darkens innocence and continually initiates us into the gritty realities of financial exchange ... It takes us out of our innocent idealism and brings us into the deeper, more soulful places where power, prestige, and self-worth are hammered out ... Therefore, money can give grounding and grit to a soul that otherwise might fade in the soft pastels of innocence."[15] These words help to remind me that there can be a purpose to my negative money experiences.

To help others with daily insurance concerns, I show them how to outline the facts of their policy—their monthly costs, coverage, and exclusions. We then examine these facts in the context of their total financial picture to see if the insurance fits in with their other priorities. I find that once people have an understanding of their policies, costs, and finances they can work through their fears and make the necessary adjustments to meet their current needs.

In most cases people have a much harder time motivating themselves to analyze their insurance than they have in actually managing it. However, once they realize the psychological importance of having the right amount of insurance, they are more willing to examine their facts.

As I prepared for Maria's next session, I considered how I might inspire her to manage her insurance. I knew her lack of knowledge of the subject was a main reason for her anxiety and resistance, so I made up several sheets of insurance facts which would help her understand her insurance.

MARIA'S TENTH SESSION

"Well, Maria, today I thought we'd talk about insurance." This was my opening gambit, and I hoped that she'd be receptive to it.

"Okay," Maria replied, and by the unenthusiastic look she gave me I could see that it was going to be a challenge.

"Have you purchased insurance before?"

"Not really. I had medical insurance when I was in the Peace Corps, but it was given to me by the government, and my car is owned by my mother so I didn't have to buy car insurance."

"And you don't have any life insurance or tenant's insurance?"

"No."

"Okay, so we have to start from scratch."

"I guess so."

We sat in silence for several moments as I thought about how I should approach this topic. I decided that the best way was to confront the anxieties it created.

"You know, Maria, most people are afraid to look at their insurance policies. I was talking to an insurance agent yesterday, and he said that every day he gets at least one call from a client who is unable to deal with his insurance because he has never read his policy."

"I can imagine. It's a scary subject."

"Why do you think that is?"

"I don't know." Maria paused and thought for a minute. "It's complicated and seems so unnecessary."

"You're right," I smiled at Maria. "It can be hard to understand. And I think people consider it unnecessary until they're told they have to have it. It's an intangible cost one doesn't anticipate."

"And it can be very expensive!" Maria exclaimed.

"Yes, and that frightens people." Again we sat in silence. I decided that it was time to share why I buy insurance.

"I never thought much about insurance until I realized the psychological protection it could provide me. Just knowing I have insurance gives me peace of mind."

These words caught Maria's attention. "So there is a real psychological connection?" she asked.

"I think there is," I replied. "I'm paying over $300 per month for our medical insurance, and for the last two years we've never claimed as much as we've spent. Yet I'm thankful to have this insurance since I wouldn't be able to sleep at night if I didn't have it. For me having insurance is a psychological necessity."

"I understand," Maria remarked.

"Now when people buy more insurance than they can afford, I'm afraid they may be suffering from feelings of insecurity."

"I never thought of that," Maria commented with a smile.

"I had to when counseling people on their life insurance. So many purchase more than they need." I paused, and then added, "Usually it's because they let their anxieties and not their finances determine the amount they buy."

"That must be a problem," Maria said.

"It is," I agreed and shook my head. "I don't have an answer to it, but I do try to get people to think about what it means for them to be really secure." I waited a while and then added, "Most admit it is not about having money or insurance."

"What is it about then?" Maria asked.

"Usually they say it has to do with how much they believe in themselves," I replied.

"I agree with that," Maria remarked.

"In any case," I continued, "once they make that acknowledgment, they seem to be better at detaching themselves from their need for so much insurance. Then I can help them choose an amount they can afford."

"I guess I'll have to psychoanalyze myself before I buy insurance," Marie said, laughing.

"That's right," I replied with a smile. "But first you need to understand how it works."

We took a short break. When Maria returned, I spread out my sheets of information on insurance and started right in. "Let's talk about the different types of insurance and how they work," I suggested.

"Okay," Maria answered.

"There are four basic kinds of insurance: home, car, health, and life. I'll start with the home."

"Fine."

"Home protection has three major parts to it. First, there is personal liability—that is, claims others make as a result of accidents or injuries on your premises. Do you follow me?"

"Yes."

"The second is home protection. This is insurance against damages that may occur to your home and property. Okay?"

"I'm with you."

"The last part is personal property protection—protection against losses or damage to your personal possessions. There may also be some minor medical payments on accidents on the premises, but that's usually a small part of the total package."

"Okay."

"If you are renting your home, you just need the liability and the personal property insurance since your landlord covers the home protection."

"I understand." I could tell that Maria really was following me. I took a moment to get two sheets of facts from my desk. I held the sheets as I continued talking.

"Now the best way to go about purchasing this home insurance is to draw up a simple information form of facts which you can use as a guide for selecting the one you want. I made a sheet for you." I handed the sheet to Maria and kept a copy for myself.

"Thanks," Maria said, as she scanned it.

"I also have similar fact sheet forms for your car, medical, and life insurance. Before choosing your insurance, I would get these facts from several companies and compare what they offer. I would also get someone who has experience with insurance to help you make your choice."

"I like that idea. I don't think I could do it myself."

"I think it's always wise to have help in making these decisions." I paused and looked at the sheet I had in my hand.

"Let me explain these facts on home insurance.

"At the top I listed the total annual and monthly cost of the insurance. These are essential to know."

"Okay."

"Next under *Home Protection* I put *the replacement value of your home* to help you estimate the amount of insurance you need, *the minimum required protection* you must have as normally dictated by state law, *the amount of protection* the policy will give you, *its cost,* and *the amount that is deductible*—that is, the amount that won't be covered. Do these facts make sense?"

"Yes."

"I also listed the specific *items covered* and *excluded* in the policy."

"Yes, I see."

"Okay. Next, under the *Personal Property* part I put *the value of possessions, the amount of insurance* covered under the policy, its *cost,* and its *deductible.*"

I paused to give Maria time to digest the facts we had gone over. I was almost finished. There were only two items left on the sheet: *personal liability*—that is, the protection from suits from others—and *medical payments.* I was pleased at how receptive Maria was to this sheet. I continued.

"The last items are *Personal Liability* and *Medical Payments.* Under *Personal Liability* I included the *amount* and its *cost.* And under *Medical Payments,* you can note the *payments the company offers* and the *amounts.* Usually there is no separate charge for medical payments."

Maria took another few minutes to study this sheet. Then she filed it in her notebook.

We paused, and I got another sheet of facts from my desk.

"The next type of insurance you will eventually need is car insurance."

"Yes. When I get the car in my name, I'll have to have it," Maria acknowledged.

"When you do, you can use this sheet of facts to help you shop for your insurance." I handed Maria a copy of the sheet I had made up on car insurance. As she looked at it, I began to explain the general format of a car insurance policy.

"Like home insurance there are also three main parts to this policy: personal liability, which is protection against suits from others; personal property, protection from thefts of items like car radios and damages to car windows, etc.; and collision, protection against damages to your car in accidents or collisions. Are you familiar with these terms?"

"Yes, but I don't know much about them."

"Personal liability refers to protection against accidents affecting others. Okay?"

"Yes."

"Personal property refers to protection against theft and

damage to your car parts." I paused and Maria nodded her head so I continued, "And collision refers to protection against damages to your car caused by a collision."

"I think I have it."

"Okay. Let's go over the facts for car insurance." I looked at my copy of facts. "Again I start with the *total monthly and annual costs.*"

"Good."

"Then under *Personal Liability* I list *the coverage* and *the cost.* The coverage can seem high. It can go up to $1 million, but there is usually a minimum requirement under state law which is much less. To determine the amount, you'll have to see what you can afford. Under *Personal Property* and *Collision,* I indicate *the coverage, the cost,* and *the deductible.* At the bottom I put *other benefits.* Again you'll have to judge how much insurance you can afford."

Maria looked over the sheet, then asked, "Do I have to have collision insurance?"

"You don't have to have collision insurance. It covers only your car."

"My father told me that personal liability insurance covered the cost of fixing up the other person's car if we have an accident."

"That's right, but it wouldn't cover your car."

"But wouldn't the other person's liability insurance cover my car."

"Not necessarily. If the accident is your fault, his insurance might not cover it."

"I see."

"And he might not be insured."

"That's right."

"Of course, if you damage your car by running into a fence, you wouldn't be covered unless you had collision insurance. Usually it's good to have collision insurance unless your car is so old or battered that it isn't worth repairing."

"I'd want my car covered at least for now."

"Yes. That makes sense, since the car your mother just bought is in good condition."

We paused and I waited to see if Maria had any more questions about this sheet. She didn't, so I continued.

"The next major type of insurance I'm sure you'll need, if you don't already have it, is medical insurance." I paused here to give Maria time to switch her thoughts to this next insurance.

"I will have to get it soon," Maria said. "Right now I'm still on the government's plan, but that ends in the next few months. I don't know what I'll do then. Getting individual insurance is expensive."

"There are a lot of plans available, and I'm sure you can find one that you can afford. You'll probably have to take a large deductible, but that's all right as long as it insures you against major illnesses and operations. There are group plans you can join which are always cheaper than individual plans. I'm in a chamber of commerce plan which has been good for me."

"I'll have to look into them."

"Here's another sheet of facts to help you decide which plan to choose." I handed her the sheet.

"This sheet has *the total annual and monthly cost; the period of coverage; the amount of the deductible for an individual or family; the way the deductible is calculated (either for each illness or for illnesses for the whole year); the amount for which you are co-insured with the company after meeting the deductible;* and *the maximum out-of-pocket expenses* you will have to pay before the company covers you at 100%. Do these make sense?"

"Yes. I understand them."

"After these deductions I list *insurance benefits the company might offer—accident benefits, out-of-pocket expenses, life insurance,* and *child age protection.*" Maria was following me on her list as I went down my list. I stopped and said, "You will want to ask the company what other benefits they pay."

"Okay," Maria replied.

"The other facts you need to ask about are the items covered under the policy and the exclusions. I would make a list of each."

"Okay."

"That does it for health insurance. It isn't that complicated if you know the facts to ask about. Do you have any questions about this list?"

"Not now. I'm sure I will have when I start looking."

"You can ask your friends who have insurance."

"I will." We stopped here for a moment, and I took out the last sheet I had.

"Now the last major type of insurance is life insurance. I assume you don't have this insurance?"

"No. I can't say it interests me either."

"It doesn't interest many people, but some really need it."

"I don't."

"Not now. But if you had a child and were the only source of support, you would want insurance to protect your child if you died."

"Yes, I guess I would."

"Then it's worth knowing about."

"Okay."

"There are two basic kinds of life insurance—*ordinary or whole life* and *term* insurance."

"I've heard those terms."

"*Ordinary Life* insures you for as long as you live. You pay an annual premium. Part of this premium goes into a reserve which you can borrow against. As this reserve grows over the years, your insurance acquires a cash surrender value. When you have paid in enough premiums to cover your insurance, your policy is paid up and its cash surrender value is equal to your total insurance."

"Then it is also a savings plan!" Maria exclaimed. "A friend of mine said it was, but I wasn't sure."

"Yes, it is, but a pretty expensive one, as a good amount

of your premium goes to pay for your life insurance. In the first years very little goes into the savings reserve."

"I see."

I paused and waited to see if Maria had any more thoughts about this insurance. She said nothing, so I continued.

"That's an overall view of ordinary life. Do you think you can remember it?"

"I think so."

"Okay. The other basic insurance is *term insurance.*"

"I know a little about that," Maria interjected. "My friend told me about her group term insurance at her company. That's insurance for a fixed number of years, isn't it?"

"Yes. Often up to age seventy." Again you pay an annual premium, but you get no savings build-up or cash surrender value as you do with *Ordinary Life.*"

"It's cheaper than the other insurance, right?"

"Yes. In the earlier years, it can be much cheaper. However, in the later years it can be more expensive as the premiums increase with your age."

"That's why they try to sell me so much insurance now when I'm young. It's so cheap."

"Exactly."

Since Maria was being so receptive to this information, I decided to bring in one other insurance concept.

"Besides *Ordinary Life* and *Term Life,* there is another basic product that insurance companies sell—*Annuities.*" I paused here to see if Maria understood the term. She gave me a blank expression, so I went on with my explanation.

"*Annuities* are forced savings plans for retirement. In such a plan you pay in a certain amount either in a lump sum or installments, and the company invests your money and guarantees you a minimal annual rate of interest, say 8%, on your money until you retire or reach retirement age. This interest is reinvested each year by the insurance company. When you retire, you receive your investment back plus the accumulated interest either in a lump sum or in installments. Do you understand?"

"Yes. Does it include life insurance with it?" Maria asked.

"Most plans offer life insurance, but you usually don't have to buy it."

"Why would I want an annuity?"

"To save money for retirement. The advantage of buying an annuity is that you don't have to pay income taxes on the interest earned until you retire."

"I couldn't use it now since I have no money to invest."

"No. But sometime you may. You ought to know there are several disadvantages to these plans. Once you've invested your money in an annuity, you normally can't get it out until retirement and you can't borrow against it. And the plans are not cheap to get into."

Again I paused to see if Maria had questions. She didn't, so I summed up my brief description of life insurance.

"So now you know the three main products life insurance companies offer—*Ordinary Life, Term Life,* and *Annuities.* They have many variations of these products, but if you have a basic understanding of how these three work, you can understand them. I also have a sheet of facts you can follow." I handed Maria her copy of the information sheet I'd made up on life insurance.

"Good," Maria commented, as she scanned the paper.

"You see that I've included *the annual and monthly cost, type and amount of insurance, time of coverage, cost, accumulated savings reserve, cash surrender value, interest rate* you would earn on your savings reserve or annuity, *borrowing rate* if you borrowed from your savings reserve, annual payments of *dividends* or *capital* that the insurance company might give you, *annuity payments* when you retire, *death benefits* if you die, any *conversion options*—options the company has to convert from one type of insurance to another, and any *other options* the company may offer."

Maria reviewed the facts as I mentioned them. She didn't

seem to be daunted by them. When I had finished, she filed the sheet along with the others.

"That completes what I wanted to give you on insurance. The information sheets will help you select your insurance. To determine the amount of insurance you need, I suggest that you draw up a summary of your finances (see p. 237) and budget your cost."

"Okay."

"Be sure to have someone knowledgeable in insurance help you make your decisions."

"I will," Maria said, as she turned to go out the door.

As she was about to get into her car, I shouted a last parting thought.

"And do your psychoanalysis!" Maria nodded her head and smiled.

* * *

Most people don't have the guidelines for buying insurance that I gave Maria, and so they are at the mercy of the insurance agents and their own anxieties.

GRACE

A designer named Grace came to me because she was having trouble meeting her bills. When she reviewed her expenses, she was appalled to find that she was spending more money on her insurance than on her food!

"I must be overly neurotic," she exclaimed.

"No, the life insurance salesperson just caught you at an anxious moment," I replied with a laugh.

I was right. We reviewed her life insurance and found that she had bought a $200,000 *Ordinary Life* insurance policy right after her husband had left her. This insurance cost her thousands of dollars more than she could afford. She had bought this insurance through a friend who had been kind to her while she was going through the divorce. At the time she was feeling so lonely and depressed that she hadn't considered the financial consequences of her purchase. She was just grateful for his support. Now as she looked at her insurance expense, she became angry at what she had let herself be talked into.

I asked Grace if she had talked to her friend about her financial situation. She said no, she hadn't. Then I said he wasn't responsible for selling her too much insurance since he didn't know that she couldn't afford it. She agreed. She admitted that she might be overly judgmental. As she thought it over, she remembered that at the time she had wanted as much insurance as she could get. She had no job and was fearful that her two little children would have nothing if she died.

I told Grace that her friend might have sold her *Term Insurance* which would have been much cheaper, but he was probably trying to help her do some forced savings by having her buy the *whole life*, knowing that part of her premium would go into a savings reserve.

I advised Grace to forgive him, if she possibly could, since holding resentment would undermine their relationship and her peace of mind. In the future she would know better than to buy insurance without knowing how much she could afford.

She said that she wanted to forgive him, but she didn't know if she could continue working with him. I mentioned that I thought she could now that she understood her finances well enough to tell him what she wanted.

"Won't he be upset if I ask him to reduce my insurance?" she asked.

"That's his choice," I replied. "If he's a real friend, he'll understand your predicament." Grace said she'd give it some thought, and we dropped the subject and moved on to analyzing her current life insurance needs.

Now that she was working and felt much more secure,

she decided to cancel her *Ordinary Life* policy and buy $100,000 of *Term Insurance*. By making this switch, she would save more than $3,000 in premiums per year. She knew that this would reduce her insurance by $100,000, but she wasn't afraid to do it because she was on much friendlier terms with her ex-husband now, and he had assured her that he would take care of the children if anything happened to her.

Once this insurance concern had been resolved, we looked at Grace's other insurance and discovered several changes she could make to better her position. She could improve her home protection by getting her valuable possessions appraised and covered under her policy. She could save on the costs of her auto insurance by removing the collision protection on her ten-year-old Ford, which was in her words "beyond redemption." And she could switch her individual medical insurance to a cheaper group plan.

These changes were easy for Grace to make. However, they required her having the will to do them. It wasn't I who inspired her. It was her recognition of what her own anxiety had cost her that spurred her into action.

In dealing with insurance we tend to avoid it, live in fear of it, and let others tell us how much we need. As Grace found out, this attitude can cost us friendship, money, and security.

We know that our real protection in life is not based on how much insurance we have but on our own inner strength. To maintain this strength we need to examine our insurance in the context of our finances and personal values and choose a policy that is appropriate to our actual needs.

* * *

Exercises:

1. Before buying insurance, draw up a summary of your finances (see p. 237), and use this summary as a guide to decide how much insurance you can afford to buy.

2. Before making any insurance decision, meditate on it. If you have any doubts about it, hold off until you're sure it feels right for you.

3. Make up information sheets for your home, car, health, and life insurance using the following facts. Let these guides help you in selecting your insurance.

*   *   *

Home Insurance

A. Total annual and monthly cost

B. Under Home Protection
   a. replacement value of home
   b. minimum protection required
   c. amount of protection
   d. cost
   e. deductible
   f. items covered
   g. items excluded

C. Under Personal Property
   a. value of possessions
   b. amount of insurance
   c. cost
   d. deductible

D. Under Personal Liability
   a. amount of insurance
   b. cost

E. Under medical payments
   a. types of payments
   b. amounts

* * *

Car Insurance

A. Personal Liability
   a. coverage
   b. cost

B. Personal Property
   a. coverage
   b. cost
   c. deductible

C. Collision
   a. coverage
   b. cost
   c. deductible

D. Other benefits

*   *   *

Health Insurance

A. General Information
   a. total annual cost
   b. total monthly cost
   c. period of coverage
   d. deductible—individual/family
      per illness—per year
   e. co-insurance obligation
   f. maximum out-of-pocket expenses

B. Insurance Benefits
   a. accident benefits
   b. out-of-pocket expenses
   c. life insurance
   d. child age protection

C. Items Covered

D. Items Excluded

* * *

Life Insurance

A. Type of Insurance
    a. Ordinary (Whole) Life
    b. term
    c. annuity
    d. other options

B. General Information
    a. amount of insurance
    b. annual cost
    c. time of coverage
    d. changes in cost
    e. interest rate on savings reserve
    f. borrowing rate
    g. annual dividends
    h. capital distributions
    i. annuity payments
    j. death benefits
    k. conversion options
    l. other options

*   *   *

12

Sharing the Burden

Taxes

MOST PEOPLE know the importance of sharing, but getting them to understand why they have to share the burden of paying taxes is another matter. Many are so negative about their taxes that they will give up almost anything to avoid them. I remember a friend who gave up a meaningful relationship because of a capital gains tax.

My friend had formed a close attachment to a retired man who lived in New Hampshire. Since she lived in Maine, they had to go back and forth between states to see each other. As their relationship deepened, they considered selling one of their homes and living together. However, when they looked at the tax consequences, they discovered that the capital gains taxes either one would have to pay would be so large that neither thought he or she could afford to sell. So they held on to their properties and continued seeing each other from a distance. Eventually, however, the commutes were too much for them, and the relationship ended.

For me, the sad part of the story was that I knew, from the previous consulting I had done with my friend, that she could afford to sell her home and move to New Hampshire. She had plenty of savings to pay the capital gains tax and more than enough income to support herself for the rest of her life wherever she lived. Yet I also knew that my friend was very anxious about her money and had a real fear of paying taxes. When she told me that she wouldn't pay the capital gains tax, she gave me such a determined look that I knew there was no hope of changing her mind. She acted as if she had no other choice but to avoid the tax. Whether she knew her decision would ultimately break up the relationship, I don't know, but her fear was so great at that moment that I don't think she could have listened to her heart even if she had wanted to. When she later told me that she had broken up with the man, she looked so crestfallen that I was sure she now regretted her decision to stay in Maine.

I considered telling my friend that it wasn't the commute that caused the relationship to end, it was her unwillingness to pay the capital gains tax. But I decided against it, as I felt it wouldn't do any good and it might hurt our friendship.

*   *   *

In my early years of paying taxes, I started out with many of the same fears as my friend had. I think part of my attitude came from my father who, as a self-made man and successful wage earner, was taxed heavily. Although philosophically he agreed that we needed to pay taxes, he resented the amount he was taxed and worried about being able to meet these obligations.

My father's feelings stayed with me until Ram forced me to reassess my negative attitude. Ram Dass, a.k.a. Richard Alpert, was a Harvard professor, who in 1967 went to India to study Eastern spiritualism. He returned to this country and is now a lecturer, writer, and founder of numerous projects designed to increase spiritual consciousness in the West.

In his thoughts about giving service, Ram Dass helped me to find a new purpose for my taxes—one which made me more responsible. *How Can I Help?* by Ram Dass and Paul Gorman[16] states that providing service to others is an important part of our journey back to oneness as it is a way to overcome our separateness, which is the basis for many of our fears. In doing service we "meet behind our separateness" and share the experience of unity.

This seemed to me a very good analogy of what paying taxes was about. My tax money was going to help support public concerns and our social infrastructure. In this respect it was another way of getting past the separateness I felt with those in our larger community. By supporting them through public funds I was indirectly sharing an experience of unity.

At first I wasn't comfortable with this idea because I often didn't approve of how the federal and state governments spent my money. Upon further reflection, I realized from a spiritual perspective my approval or disapproval wasn't important, only the service I was rendering. I had a responsibility to share the tax burden and accept the imperfections of those who administered my funds.

These are thoughts I try to share with others when I help them plan their income taxes. At the same time, I have them write down their income, deductions, credits, tax payments, and other pertinent facts for calculating what they owe. I then help them estimate their taxes and show them how they can legally reduce them. If they haven't paid in enough to cover their taxes, I help them set up a plan for putting aside the money they will need.

Over the years I've found that people have three main problems dealing with income taxes: they hate the IRS, they fail to take the right amount of deductions, and they fail to make sufficient payments.

For those who see the IRS as their enemy, I tell them my one and only experience with this government agency.

I was living in Philadelphia when I received a letter from the IRS stating that I had to have my income taxes reviewed. Terrified by the prospect, I hired a lawyer to come with me. We went to the IRS office and I was directed to an older man sitting in the back. Without looking at me, he took my tax return and began to examine it. He looked up abruptly and smiled. "Do you know Betty Lang?" he asked.

"Sure," I replied, a little confused. "She lives right next door to me. She's a good neighbor."

"She's a great person," he said, and for the next several minutes we talked about Betty and her family, and I told him how she had brought us our first meal while we were painting the house. The man's attitude became very friendly toward me, and when he looked again at my tax returns, he didn't comment on them. He just picked them up and handed them to me saying, "I'm sure everything's okay."

We shook hands, and I walked out. As we got to the elevator, my lawyer said laughingly, "You didn't need me in this interview; you had Betty Lang!"

People like my story, as it shows there is a human side to the IRS which they tend to forget in their concern over their taxes.

The other two problems, failing to take the right deductions and not making enough payments, are best illustrated by the case of a high-powered computer consultant named Doug.

DOUG

Doug asked for my help because he was worried about how much he was paying in income taxes. He had a very good business, but most of his profits were going to the IRS.

We reviewed Doug's business and decided that he was making enough money that he could afford to set up a Self-Employment Retirement Plan (S.E.P.). Under this plan he could contribute about $7,000 and reduce his taxable income by a similar amount. This would save him over $2,000 in federal and state income taxes for the coming tax year. Doug liked this plan, but wasn't sure how he would come up with such a large contribution.

I suggested that every month Doug put a portion of the money he received from his consulting into a fund reserved for his S.E.P. If he planned to put $7,000 in his S.E.P. this year, he might put 1/12 of that amount or about $583 per month. He could invest this money in a Money Market Fund until he was ready to transfer it to his S.E.P. If he found he couldn't afford to put this amount in, he was under no obligation to do so, and if he needed extra money for his business, he could take it back from the reserve fund. He didn't have to put money in his S.E.P. until April 15.

Doug agreed to try this. He then asked me what he should do about paying his income taxes since he was always having trouble meeting his quarterly payments. I advised him to put a monthly amount in the reserve fund along with the S.E.P. money. He could write checks against the Money Market Fund to cover his quarterly payments. He liked that idea, too, so we had to work up an estimate of the amount of tax he would owe and the amount he would put in the fund each month.

As I was going over Doug's 1040 Form to calculate these amounts, I noticed he hadn't included his state income taxes when he listed his deductions. I asked him why he hadn't done so. He said he didn't know that he could. I explained that if he paid them before December 31, he could deduct them.

Doug was concerned that his accountant hadn't told him about this. He said that he had understood he had to pay his state income tax on April 15. I told him that this year he should remember to pay it before the end of December.

We left the matter there, and I reviewed Doug's sales and expenses on his Schedule C Form and found that, based on his taxable annual income (adjusted for the payments into S.E.P.), he should pay about $2,000 a month into his reserve fund to cover his taxes. Again if he needed the money, he could always take it back.

A year later in March I returned to review Doug's progress. He said that he had had a good year. He had changed tax accountants, having consolidated his tax and bookkeeping work under one service. He had kept up with his S.E.P. and tax payments, but since he made more than in the previous year, he still owed about $1,000 more to the IRS and $5,500 to the state.

I asked Doug why he didn't pay the state before December 31 as I had suggested. He said that he had called his bookkeeper in December and asked if he could take the deduction and she said she wasn't sure, but she would talk to the tax accountant who worked with her. She had never gotten back to Doug, and he had let it go.

We decided to call his tax accountant directly to see if he could have taken the deduction. The accountant said that Doug could have taken the deduction, but in December when Doug called they didn't know that, because they weren't sure if he would be itemizing his deductions or taking the standard deduction. If he took the standard deduction, he wouldn't be able to take off the state tax payments.

I asked the tax accountant why he didn't know that Doug was itemizing his deductions, and he said that Doug and his wife filed separate returns and used separate accountants, and they hadn't found out from Doug's wife whether she was itemizing her deductions or taking the standard deduction. If Doug's wife took the standard deduction, Doug had to take the standard deduction. If his wife itemized, he would have to itemize.

Doug and I were disappointed that this hadn't been clarified in December, but we knew nothing could be done about it now. We calculated that Doug would not have owed the IRS $1,000 if he had been able to deduct the state income tax payments.

Doug realized that there was a lesson to be learned from this experience and that he was at fault for not having found out what he should have done. In years past, he had never taken charge of his taxes. He had passively let the accountants tell him what he owed and never reviewed their work. Now he knew he had to take responsibility for these obligations.

When I teach classes on managing taxes, I use Doug as an example; I then urge students to consider taxes from a spiritual perspective: If they can bless them, they won't be resistant to paying them.

SHIRLEY

The idea of "blessing taxes" always creates a controversy, as many of the students hate paying taxes or supporting the government. One student, named Shirley, shared a particularly difficult experience with the IRS in which she was directly penalized when the company she owned was thrown into bankruptcy for getting behind on its tax payments. Although the company settled its debts with the IRS, the IRS still put a lien on all Shirley's personal property, and because of that Shirley was extremely bitter.

I asked Shirley if she could think of anything positive that had come from this experience.

After some thought she said that there had been one good thing. The experience had brought her closer to her husband. She explained that it was partially due to his negligence that the taxes were never paid. She had been assigned to work away from the company office where her husband worked. In doing her business, she had realized that some taxes weren't being paid and had notified her husband that there was a managerial problem. Her husband had assured her he had taken care of it when, in fact, he hadn't. Then the business manager went on vacation and never returned. When an outside accountant went through the company's books, he found that the company owed over $30,000 of overdue taxes, which the business manager had never paid.

When Shirley found out what had happened, she considered divorcing her husband. Instead she confronted him with her feelings, and he accepted the responsibility for what he had done. Together they worked through the bankruptcy and kept their relationship intact. However, they did mutually agree not to go into business together again.

In telling us this part of the story, Shirley had to admit that there had been a positive side to the experience, since she had developed a better understanding of her husband and their life together.

I reminded Shirley and the rest of the class that there were always human issues in every money problem, and addressing these issues was just as important as dealing with the money concerns.

What Maria's issues were with taxes I didn't know, but as she was one of those in the class who rebelled against blessing them, I expected our next session on taxes would be a challenge.

MARIA'S ELEVENTH SESSION

In this session I was going to help Maria understand her income taxes as well as find the motive for paying them. Knowing how difficult this subject was, I decided to make up another fact sheet with tax information for her. It happened that the time of this session was a week before income taxes were due, so I started off asking Maria about these taxes.

"Have you done your income taxes, Maria?" I asked.

"No. I always wait until the last moment," Maria replied. "I hate doing these taxes."

I said nothing as I considered how I should proceed. Maria's mentioning the word *hate* reminded me of a statement by a yoga teacher that I thought would be an appropriate beginning.

"Maria, I was listening to a tape by a yoga teacher yesterday, and he said that every time you say you hate something, you lose energy. I think we do waste a lot of energy being negative about things like taxes."

"I suppose we do. I hadn't thought of it in that way."

"In my counseling I see many people who rant and rave about having to pay their taxes, and I can visibly see how much the subject exhausts them."

"Do you think it affects their health?" Maria asked.

"It doesn't do their health any good," I replied. "I think the stress of taxes may cause many illnesses. I know it causes a lot of people to lose sleep."

"I bet," Maria replied, and we both chuckled.

"The reality is we only pay taxes when we own property and make money, so the obligation is contingent on our being prosperous."

"I guess you're right. From that point of view taxes aren't all that bad," Maria conceded.

"I like to think of my taxes as a way of sharing my money with those in the larger community. I know this is idealistic and that our taxes are unfairly distributed and often misspent, but I feel that living with an ideal like this is part of my spiritual life—and it keeps me honest," I said with a smile.

"So again it's a spiritual issue." There was no surprise in Maria's voice as she had heard this from me many times before.

"Yes, I believe it is. I think that paying taxes is a spiritual commitment just like paying our debts. I don't think we can treat any of our finances as if they were separate from us. They certainly affect how we feel—especially taxes."

"You have a good point," Maria acknowledged.

We paused, and I dropped the subject. I thought it was time to give Maria some basic tax information.

"Let's now look at the facts you need to calculate your taxes. We'll start with income taxes, since that's the one you have to deal with this next week."

"Okay."

I handed Maria a copy of the tax information sheet I had made up.

"Here's another sheet of facts you can use as a guide."

"Thanks." She took the sheet and glanced briefly at it.

"Let's go over the facts you'll need."

"Okay."

"Since you have no dependents, you may be able to use a simpler form than the usual 1040 Form. This year they have two alternative forms: the 1040 EZ, which is just one page, and 1040 A, which is two pages."

"I was told to use the 1040 Form because I have my own business."

"Okay. Are you going to do your own taxes?"

"I don't know. This is the first time I had a business, which makes it more complicated. The other times I just had my government salary, and it was simple."

"I would get some help. The 1040 Form can be tricky."

"Okay."

"However, before you go to anyone, I would write down the tax information you'll need. This sheet will help you." I looked down at the sheet.

"The first item is your *Income.* Did you receive any wages this year?"

"Yes. When I was waitressing."

"Do you have your W-2 Form?"

"Yes."

"Then put the total income from wages down."

"Okay."

"Now, what other income did you receive that's not from your business?"

"I got a little savings interest."

"Okay, put that amount down."

"Anything else?"

"Nothing except the money from the Spanish lessons I give."

"That's the business you're in?"

"Yes."

"Before you can include what you received from your lessons, you need to add up the amount you received during the year and subtract your expenses. I would list the expenses on another sheet. You will need to give them to your tax person. He or she will have to include this information on a Schedule C Form which goes in with your 1040 Form."

"Okay."

"On your information sheet you'll want to include the net amount you received after all your expenses. It may not be completely accurate since your tax person will probably find a few additional expenses you can subtract, but it will give you a good estimate."

"I think I can do that," Maria said, "although my records aren't very good."

"I understand. I don't keep very good records either, but I find that if I write checks for all my business expenses, I can usually identify them from my checkbook records."

"I'll have to try that." Maria made a note to herself to use checks for all business expenses. I waited until she was finished.

"Once you have all your income down, you go to the next item on the sheet which is *Exemptions.*"

"I see." Maria looked again at her sheet.

"You can claim yourself as one exemption. Since this year

each exemption is $2,350, you can subtract that amount from your income. Do you follow me?"

"Yes."

"The next item is *Deductions*. The standard deduction, if you are single, is $3,700."

"So I can subtract that amount, too?"

"Right. If you have more than $3,700 worth of deductions, you would itemize them."

"I don't have that," Maria said.

"Then you use the standard deduction."

I paused to give her a chance to get into a more comfortable position. When she was settled, I continued.

"Once you've subtracted your *Exemption* and *Deduction*, you're left with your *Taxable Income*. Now you can look up in the IRS tax book and see the amount of *Federal Income Tax* you owe. Here, I have a book with me." I showed Maria the book with the tax table. I showed her the taxable income table in bold letters and the corresponding tax below it. To show her how to read it, I pointed to the taxable income of $23,000.

"If you have a taxable income of $23,000 and you are single, you owe $3,574."

"I see," Maria replied.

I looked at the next category. "If you were married, filing jointly, you would owe $3,454—a little less."

"The book's easy to read," Maria commented.

I put the book down and returned to the fact sheet.

"Yes, it is. And once you have your tax amount, all you have to do is subtract any *Tax Credits* you have, and you will have the *Net Amount* you will owe."

"What are credits?" Maria asked.

"They are special expenses that you can subtract directly from your tax. One such credit is for child- and dependent-care expenses."

"I don't think I have any credits."

"Probably not, but you might in the future."

I stopped and before going to the next item, *Payments,* I asked Maria, "Have you paid any additional money to the IRS besides the amounts that were deducted from your wages?"

"No. I didn't think I had to."

"You're supposed to make quarterly payments on income other than the taxes deducted from your paycheck."

"Oh!" Maria exclaimed, and I could see that she was upset.

"Have you made much money from your Spanish lessons?" I asked.

"Not much. I'd say about $5,000."

"Then you probably don't have anything to worry about. The IRS rules can change every year, but currently at lower levels of income one has to pay 90% of the taxes one owes in the current year by January 15 of the following year; or, at least, the same amount as one paid in the previous year."

"I didn't pay much in the previous year," Maria said. "I didn't have my business."

"Then you should have no problem," I replied.

"That's good."

I paused again as Maria visibly relaxed in her chair. It had been a tense moment—one that many of my clients face who avoid making payments on the income they received outside of their normal wages.

I turned again to the fact sheet where I had included *Income Tax Payments.* I began to explain them to Maria.

"The next item on your sheet is *Tax Payments.* You need to write down the amount of income taxes that were deducted from your annual wages as a waitress. It's on your W-2 Form."

"Okay."

"If you had made any *Other Payments,* you'd include them."

"Yes."

"Then you subtract your *Payments* from *the amount of*

tax you owe to see what you still must pay; or, if you over-paid, the *tax credit* that is owed you."

"I understand."

"Good. Calculating federal income taxes can be compli-cated. This sheet just gives you a simple overview to help you organize your facts. Your tax person will have to trans-late these facts onto your 1040 Form. But if you use this sheet, you will save your tax person time, which will save you money."

"I like that," Maria said.

We took a short break before going on to the next item on the sheet, *State Income Taxes.* When we started again, Maria picked up her sheet, and I continued from where we had left off.

"The next item, *State Income Taxes,* is usually simpler to calculate. You take the *Total Taxable Income* on your 1040 Federal Income Tax Form and add any *Non-allowable De-ductions* in order to get your *Total State Income.*"

"What are *Non-allowable Deductions?*" Maria asked.

"They are items that you can deduct or exclude from your federal income, but you can't from state income." I searched in my mind for a good example. "Certain income one re-ceives from municipal bonds is not included as part of your *Federal Income,* but has to be included as part of your *State Income.*"

"How will I know what should be included?"

"Your tax person will tell you."

"Good." Maria looked relieved.

"Any other questions?"

"No."

"Then I'll go on. Once you've established your *State In-come,* you subtract any *State Deductions* to come up with your *State Income Tax.*"

"The tax person will have to tell me my *State Deductions,*" Maria interjected.

"Yes. And he will calculate your *State Income Tax* from

the state tax booklet he has."

"Then I don't have to give this tax person any more tax information."

"Usually not. The information for calculating your *Federal Income Taxes* is normally all the tax person needs to calculate your *State Income Taxes.* There may be cases when it isn't, but I don't think they would apply to you. I paused as I saw Maria look out the window. I gently asked, "Are you still with me?"

"Yes," she said sheepishly. I continued.

"The only other information you have to supply is your *State Tax Payments,* which include the total amount deducted from your wages on your W-2 Form."

"Okay. Should I also have made quarterly payments last year?"

"I don't know. It depends on the state you live in. In New Mexico, you don't; in New York, you do. You'll have to check with your state."

"I will."

"That completes your state tax information. The tax person will subtract your *State Tax Payments* from your *State Income Tax* to come up with the additional *amount you owe* or any tax credit if you overpaid."

"I understand."

"You'll want your tax person to help you estimate the rest of this current year's income taxes so that you can set aside money to pay for them."

"I'll get him to give me those estimates. Since I'm in school for a good part of this year, my taxes should be low."

"Then you probably won't have to make payments."

I looked at my watch. Our session was coming to a end. However, I wanted to say a few more things. I hurried on.

"There are other taxes you need to be aware of—home and property taxes, capital gains taxes, and sales taxes—but you can learn about them when you have to pay them. The hardest taxes to handle are income taxes, and the fact sheet will help you with them."

"I won't lose the sheet," Maria said, as she carefully put it in her notebook.

"I know you won't," I replied.

As Maria got up to leave, I couldn't resist giving her the standard advice I try to give everyone. "Maria, anyone can handle taxes once one learns how to plan for them. The real challenge is finding the will power to pay them. That's the spiritual hurdle you have to make."

*   *   *

Getting most clients to deal with their taxes isn't difficult, but in one case the resistance was so strong that I couldn't overcome it.

NADINE

The client's name was Nadine, and she was a very successful lobbyist for the government. For the first ten years of her business career, she had kept up with her taxes, but after she had separated from her husband, she had started to get behind on them. She had stopped paying her state income taxes, but had continued to make extra-large quarterly payments on her federal income taxes without sending in her annual 1040 Forms.

Five years later when Nadine got her tax forms in, she found that she had overpaid the government $12,000. Unfortunately, the IRS refused to return the overpayment, saying that she had delayed too long in getting her 1040s in and that the statute of limitations prevented her from receiving her money. Although she knew she had a case for contesting their decision, she had never done so.

Nadine guessed she owed over $10,000 in back state income taxes. Furthermore, she had not paid or filed her gross receipts tax during this period. (This tax was on all services done within the state; since most of her business was out of state, the amount she owed was not large, but she had to pay penalties for not filing her returns.)

For the current year Nadine was also behind on her quarterly federal income tax payment and on her property taxes.

At first it was hard for me to understand why a person like Nadine, who was talented enough to earn over $100,000 a year, couldn't get her taxes together. When she confessed that her accountant and bookkeeper had given up on her because she hadn't been able to give them the information they needed, I realized that Nadine had more than a tax problem.

I asked her why she had so much trouble with these business details, and she said they were directly tied to the emotional traumas she'd gone through. When she separated from her husband, she hadn't been able to cope with her taxes. When she had gone into therapy, she was able to get her federal income tax returns up-to-date. Then she had several other emotional entanglements that failed, and they had caused her to get behind again.

Although I felt that these experiences had adversely affected Nadine, I wasn't convinced that they were the cause of her tax problems, particularly when, during these emotional difficulties, she was able to earn so much money.

When I asked her former husband what he felt about Nadine's situation, he said that she always lived from crisis to crisis regardless of her love life. She never had had a consistent approach to her work, and it was quite typical of her to put a lot of energy into her business for a month and then let it lapse for several months.

I discussed this with Nadine, and she agreed that she had had trouble being emotionally consistent in her work, but now she was sure that she was in control of herself. I didn't disagree with her, as she was so adamant that she could cope, although I was skeptical that she could change a lifelong emotional pattern in such a short time.

The last time I heard from Nadine she canceled an appointment with me at the last moment because she said that the accountant she had recently hired hadn't completed her books; the bank was stopping her credit, since she hadn't been able to give the bank officer the tax records he required; she was going away on a two-week business and vacation trip; and she didn't know what we'd be able to accomplish in our meeting!

The point of the case is to show that we have to be totally honest about ourselves and the problems we have managing our lives if we are to deal effectively with our taxes or other finances. We can't run away from our emotional realities. We have to accept them and work with them. Only when Nadine is really able to come to terms with her emotional ups and downs can she break her crisis pattern of living and focus her energies on dealing with her money concerns.

Regardless of the kinds of emotional problems people have with taxes, I always try to get them to realize how paying these obligations can benefit their soul. When they see that it can have a spiritual purpose, they are much more motivated to pay their fair share.

*   *   *

Exercises:

1. Whenever you are worried about your income taxes, try centering yourself and doing some deep breathing to reduce your stress. (You may also want to follow the visualization exercise number 1 on page 153.) Then look at your actual tax situation and decide what you have to do to take care of your concern.

2. To plan your income taxes, make up an information sheet with the following facts as your outline:

    A. Federal Income Tax

    - a. Sources of Income
    - b. Exemptions
    - c. Deductions
    - d. Taxable Income
    - e. Federal Income Tax
    - f. Tax Credits
    - g. Federal Income Tax Payments
    - h. Tax Due or Credit

    B. State Income Tax

    - a. Total Taxable Income (taken from 1040 Form)
    - b. Non-allowable Deductions
    - c. State Income
    - d. State Deductions
    - e. State Income Tax
    - f. State Tax Payments
    - g. Tax Due or Credit

3. To prepare for filing your 1040 Federal Income Tax Form and your State Income Tax Form, fill in your information sheet first. If you aren't experienced at doing your taxes, you may want to take the information to a tax

person to have it done.

4. Keep a running estimate of your income taxes through-
    out the year, using your information sheet as a guide.

5. Try to be accepting of your taxes and conscientious
    about managing them. Think of them as a way of giving
    service to your community.

13

Choosing Your Priorities

Income and Expenses

"SHOULD WE stop buying Term Life Insurance and use that money to buy investments for our retirement?"

This was the question Mark and Jennifer presented to me when they walked into my office. They were an older couple from Albuquerque who were just beginning to focus on the retirement phase of their lives. Mark had sold his business several years ago, and Jennifer was thinking of retiring from her job the following year.

"That's an interesting question," I replied. "Before I try to answer it, we'd better look at your finances."

They agreed, and I began writing down their facts. Just as

we got started, Mark confessed he had gone through all his money gambling, playing the horses, drinking, etc. However, he assured me he had learned his lessons and was now ready to settle down.

His confession unsettled me, but I said nothing. When I asked them the value of their personal possessions, Jennifer gave me a worried look.

"I wouldn't know how much they are worth," she said rather haltingly. "We have a lot of stuff."

Mark agreed and added, "Jennifer loves to shop."

"Do you think they're worth $30,000?" I asked.

"No, I'd say $40,000," Jennifer replied, and Mark nodded his head in agreement.

I moved on to their other facts. However, Mark's revelation about his past and Jennifer's love of shopping were warning signals to me that this case might not be a simple matter of deciding whether to switch from insurance to investments.

When I completed their picture, I knew I was right. Although the couple had $20,000 in investments and owned a home and two cars, they had a sizable mortgage, costly car and credit card loans, and were overspending by roughly $400 per month or $4,800 per year. Under these circumstances, Mark and Jennifer needed to think about more than just canceling their policy. They needed to cut back on their other expenses if they hoped to save money for retirement.

I showed them the financial summary I'd drawn up and told them how much they were overspending. Jennifer said that she had been dipping into her savings to pay their bills, but she was sure they could cut back on their expenses.

We first considered their original question about getting rid of their insurance policies and buying investments. They each had $60,000 in Term Insurance, which cost a total $550 per month.

I pointed out that the insurance was expensive for them to buy at their age, and it didn't provide them with any savings reserve. They said they couldn't get any other insurance because of the health problems both of them had had.

"It's a gamble to cancel this insurance," Mark said.

"Yes, it is," I replied. "If you cancel the policies and either one of you dies, the other is left with no insurance payment."

"We know," Jennifer said. "But if I'm going to retire next year, we need some savings."

I looked at their summary again.

"What concerns me is you are already overspending by $400 per month. If you cancel your insurance and invest the $550 you save, you will still have to reduce your other expenses by $400 to get your income and expenses in balance."

"Oh! I'm sure we can do that," Mark replied, and Jennifer nodded her head in agreement.

I asked them if they were willing to sell one of their cars, since the cost of maintaining two cars was high. They said they couldn't live without them. They were, however, sure they could cut back on their spending on clothes, entertainment, and gifts. But I remembered how Mark had gone through his savings and how Jennifer loved to buy things and was skeptical they really could discipline themselves to cut these costs.

Knowing I was still dubious, Mark assured me he could make up the money they needed by working as a business consultant. Though I wanted to believe him, considering his age and his previous health problems I wasn't sure he would have the energy to start his own business.

There were also unresolved questions about Jennifer's future retirement that bothered me. Though she had $20,000 in an Individual Retirement Account, I wasn't sure that that amount plus the $550 a month they hoped to save by canceling their insurance plus her social security would be enough to make up for the job income they would lose when she retired.

Yet the two were so sincere in their belief that they could do it that I knew it wouldn't do any good to try to dissuade them from canceling the policy and investing the money. So I agreed on the condition that they cut $400 from their expenses.

As Mark and Jennifer left my office, I quietly prayed that they would be able to save the money they intended and not die in the process!

A year later I spoke with Mark, and he said that they had done everything I had asked them to do, and they were actually saving money even though he hadn't started his consulting business.

In reviewing this case, I realized how important personal objectives can be in motivating people to manage their money. Jennifer's desire to retire the following year was the spark that ignited their savings plan. While it may not have seemed realistic in light of their past spending habits, it was fueled with such determination that I was almost sure it would work.

Usually when I have people like Jennifer and Mark examine their monthly income and expenses, it helps them sort out their priorities and adjust their expenses to live within their means. For many it is a powerful therapy as it forces them to examine their lives.

Unfortunately, I find many people have a lot of resistance to examining these facts, as it makes them feel guilty to see how much money they are spending. I try to relieve them by saying that the analysis is simply a means of seeing if they are spending their money to their best interest.

"It is just another way of getting in touch with yourself," is one of my favorite lines.

I found this idea in Thich Nhat Hanh's books, *Being Peace* and *Touching Peace*.[17] Thich Nhat Hanh is a Vietnamese monk who was nominated for a Nobel Peace Prize by Martin Luther King, Jr., in 1967 for the work he did with Vietnamese refugees. He is a member of the Tiep Hien Order, and in *Being Peace* he explains what the order means. "Tiep" means to be in touch, and "in touch" translates into "in touch with one's self in order to find out the source of wisdom, understanding, and compassion in each of us."[18]

These words aptly describe what people can learn when they examine their own expenses. As they see how much they are spending on food, entertainment, gifts, personal care, clothes, and other items, they get in touch with the economic realities which help define who they are. These insights can be a source for their own self-understanding.

I remember one woman who came to see me because she never had enough money to pay her monthly bills. We examined her expenses and found that she was spending more money on entertainment than on anything else.

We discussed in which areas of entertainment this money was going, and the woman realized that she was spending most of it on dining out. I asked her if she liked to cook, and she said she did, but hadn't felt like doing it.

I explained to her that people often spend a lot on entertainment to get away from themselves, and that usually wasn't an effective remedy for what was ailing them. The woman admitted that she had been lonely since her boyfriend had left her and had been going out almost every night. We agreed that she couldn't afford this habit and, spurred on with the thought of saving money, the woman agreed to resume cooking for herself.

When several months later I unexpectedly met the woman in the food store, she said the cooking she was now doing had been very therapeutic, and she was slowly developing a healthy balance in her social life.

I didn't ask her if she was saving money, as I didn't feel that was necessary. It was enough for me to know that our simple review of her income and expenses had been the catalyst for getting her to deal more effectively with her loneliness.

Despite the valuable insights people can gain from examining their income and expenses, they will often tell me they don't want to look at them because it will force them to consider budgeting, which compromises their freedom.

I explain to these people that true freedom doesn't come from unrestrictive money management. If they want to live more independently, they can't afford to overspend since that eventually forces them to be more dependent on others.

When I decided to leave the brokerage business and become an independent financial consultant, my income was reduced in half, so I had to cut my expenses accordingly. If I hadn't lived within the budget set by my new income, I would have had to go back to working for someone else. Thus my freedom to work alone depended on my restricting my spending.

From the psychological point of view, living within a budget can be a liberating experience since it can free you from the anxiety of spending more than you have.

RAYMOND AND DANA

A couple named Raymond and Dana found this out when they were considering adding a room to their house. Dana was going to have a baby, and they felt they needed the extra space. They had an architect draw up the plans, and he estimated it would cost about $15,000 to do the job.

This was more than Raymond and Dana expected, and fearful that they might not be able to afford the expense, they came to me for advice.

We reviewed their investments and found that they had a market value of over $15,000. However, $8,000 was in an Individual Retirement Account which they couldn't touch without paying a penalty tax. That left them with $7,000 in available funds.

I advised them that $7,000 was not a large reserve for emergencies, and they acknowledged it wouldn't be appropriate to use these funds for the room.

We then looked at the value of the house they owned and the size of their current mortgage. Comparing the two, we found that they had $40,000 of equity (home ownership) value in their house. I thought that this was sufficient to qualify for a $15,000 second mortgage (or home equity loan), which is what they needed.

I explained that before they could make that decision, they would have to look at their monthly income and expenses to see if they could afford the additional loan payments.

We totaled their income and expenses and found that they were overspending by about $150 per month. I told them that if they got a second mortgage for $15,000, it would cost them over $200 per month, which would mean they would be overspending by $350 per month or $4,500 per year.

As a last resort, we reviewed each of their monthly expenses to see if any could be reduced. We found a few they could cut back on, enough to get their income and expenses in balance, but not enough to cover the additional loan payment on a second mortgage. So we had to conclude that they couldn't afford to build the room.

What fascinated me in this case is that neither Raymond nor Dana was depressed about the decision. They didn't even complain about the money they wasted on paying the architect for the plans. Immediately after giving up on the room, they began to think of ideas for dividing up their living room area to include a space for the new arrival. This possibility had always been there, but the couple had never put any thought into it. When they left me, they were on their way downtown to find some bookcases they could use as room dividers.

I can only assume from Raymond's and Dana's positive reactions that they were more worried about the costs of this project than I suspected. When the analysis of the facts confirmed what they already knew but had been unable to face, their relief overshadowed any frustration they might have had. Here was another case in which people found solace in not overcommitting themselves.

*   *   *

What Raymond and Dana and most people need is a way to monitor and set goals on their spending. In one unusual case I developed a system for doing this. It involved a gentleman who couldn't live within his means because he gave too much money away. He had so many causes which he felt bound to support, that when we went over his expenses we found that his contributions were his largest expense item. At first we tried to budget a specific amount to spend each month, but that didn't work. He was unable to stay within it since almost every month he'd find a new cause to give to.

Finally we decided that instead of trying to limit his spending on gifts, we would limit his total spending for the month by setting a specific goal. As his monthly income was $2,500, I suggested that he pencil in $2,500 in his checkbook next to his bank balance at the first of every month.

As he wrote his checks, he would subtract the amounts from the $2,500 column as well as from his bank account. If he used a credit or instant card, he would subtract those amounts also from the $2,500. In this way he could monitor how well he was living within his goal and adjust his expenses to meet it.

The gentleman tried my suggestion, and the first month he spent over his goal before the month ended. However, in the second month he was able to meet his goal by cutting back his expenses in the final week.

"I didn't like having to do it," he said, "but it forced me to live within my income and gave me the freedom to determine how I should spend my money."

Over the years I've advised many people to try this form of budgeting, and it has proven itself to be effective. For many it is much easier than trying to budget specific amounts for different categories—food, entertainment, clothes, etc.—since it provides only one goal to meet.

There is one drawback to this goal setting. If during any given month some large bills come due, one may be forced to live very simply to stay within one's spending goal.

I'm often asked how one can be prosperous if one has to budget. My answer is that budgeting is an essential step to prosperity.

As I mentioned before, prosperity is a state of mind that attracts the money and material things we need. As we apply spiritual ideals—that is, our highest pattern of thinking and acting—to our money affairs we will gain prosperity.

People who live within their means are less fearful and more open to prosperous thinking. Moreover, the discipline of budgeting seems to ground people and give them the confidence they need to attract money.

Money is a form of energy, and its inflow and outflow need to be in balance to create real prosperity.

Though I was convinced that my philosophy was right, I wasn't sure how Maria would accept it when we discussed her income and expenses in our next session together.

MARIA'S TWELFTH SESSION

"Maria, today we're going to talk about your income and expenses." These were my opening words as she settled into her chair.

"Oh, no," was Maria's immediate response. She looked very uncomfortable. I wasn't surprised at her reaction as almost everyone, including myself, finds this subject unnerving. Looking at our expenses is like looking at our own vulnerability. We hate examining our spending habits because we're afraid they will tell us things we don't want to know. I tried to console Maria.

"I know it's a difficult subject. Most people don't like it. But you need to understand your income and expenses to determine how much money you will need to borrow from your father."

"You're right, but I don't know where I've spent my money."

"You have a checkbook?"

"Yes. But I haven't kept very good records."

"That's all right. I've been doing this work for a long time, and I find that people know a lot more about their finances than they think they do. Your unconscious knows even if you don't," I laughed.

Maria relaxed, and I felt some of her resistance ebb. I continued.

"I think the hardest part about looking at expenses is the judgments we give them. We feel guilty spending money."

"I do," Maria affirmed.

"There's no need to," I replied. "It's your money, and you can do whatever you want with it."

"I know, but I worry about how I spend it."

"I worry about how I spend mine, too. But I've learned to think of examining my expenses as just another way of getting in touch with myself. It's a way to become more mindful, which the Buddhists say is essential for having peace of mind."

"I don't think it would make me peaceful," Maria replied, and there was gleam in her eye.

"It might. Mindfulness is a very powerful tool. Have you read *Touching Peace,* by Thich Nhat Hanh?"

"Yes," Maria said.

"Then you know that he thinks mindfulness is the 'seed of enlightenment,' "[19] I said.

"If you say so," Maria replied with a smile. "But he doesn't mention it in terms of money."

"No, he doesn't, but he says it's a way to transform our pain, and spending money can be painful."

"It certainly can," Maria said, and we both laughed.

"Well," I said with a chuckle, "for the good of your soul, we'd better start looking at your income and expenses."

"Okay."

"Here is the form you can use." I handed Maria the summary form (see p. 237). "You only need to fill in the income and expenses. We'll do the rest later."

Maria looked dubious. "I don't know if I can do this," she said.

"Here are some instructions." I handed Maria a sheet of instructions I had on my desk. (These are listed at the end of chapter 14, p. 231.) "This will make your work much easier."

"Okay." Maria took the sheet.

"You don't have to be exact in your estimates of these expenses, only accurate enough to make the figures meaningful."

"I'm not sure what you mean."

"If you were doing this for accounting purposes, you would need exact amounts, but when you are doing this for management purposes, you need only realistic estimates. In managing, one is more interested in the changes one needs to make, and these are easily understood by comparing approximate amounts." I paused. "Are you with me?"

"Yes."

"Good. Then I'll give you an example. If your summary showed that you were overspending by approximately $150 per month, and you were spending reasonable amounts on everything excepts gifts which were $250 per month, chances are you would try to reduce this expense. Whether you were actually spending $275 or $225 on gifts wouldn't affect your decision."

"I see."

"What you're looking for are ways to improve your position."

"Okay. That makes it more interesting."

"It is. This exercise isn't just for budgeting, although people can use it for that purpose. It's another way of learning about yourself and discovering how you can improve your life by changing spending priorities."

Maria still wasn't convinced. "I'm afraid it will tell me how badly I manage my money."

"That's only because you believe that already. The exercise merely tells you what you are doing with your money. If you don't like what you see, you can change it." I paused, then added as kindly as I could, "Remember, no judgments."

"That's hard," Maria said. "I'm so used to judging myself."

"Everyone does," I replied, "and they also assume they'll feel more helpless when they look at their expenses. But I find that they feel relieved to know where they stand. I don't think I've found anyone who felt worse after doing this exercise. Invariably people find ways for saving money and spending it more effectively."

"It would be good if I could save some money," Maria said.

"Then this exercise will help you there." I paused for a minute. There was another purpose I wanted to mention.

"But for me the most exciting part of looking at one's income and expenses is that it helps people get a little deeper into who they are. Looking at how they earn and spend their money can give them valuable insights into the nature of their personality, and changing how they direct their money can have a profound effect on how they feel about themselves."

"I suppose it can."

"I've seen the biggest changes between partners and spouses. Doing this exercise often brings them closer together, as it gives them a chance to work through many of their money differences."

"I think it could also break them apart."

"Yes, it can. But in almost all my cases it has had a healing effect. I think when couples avoid looking at their expenses, it makes it harder for them to understand each other. Often one will accuse another of spending too much without knowing the facts."

"I see what you mean."

"I think it's called Reality Therapy," I said as a joke, "and I'm afraid our time is running out so we'll have to look at your reality in our next session. Then we'll decide how much money we should ask your father for. Just fill in the summary sheet I gave you with your income and expenses, and we'll go from there."

"Okay," Maria said.

"Remember, when in doubt, always estimate on the high side for your expenses. Then you're sure to be safe."

"I will."

*　*　*

One thing I didn't tell Maria was that examining one's income and expenses can be a powerful tool for settling conflicts, especially within families. When parents and children are vying for things they need and money is short, the best way to avoid conflicts is to have parents share a summary of their monthly income and expenses with their children and show them why they can't have everything.

The parents can then use this summary as a planning guide for deciding family priorities. As I said earlier in this book, parents don't have to be afraid that their children will misuse the information they give them. Sharing these facts will bring the family closer together and make the children much less demanding and more appreciative of their situation.

In families where parents are going through a divorce, examining a summary of their monthly income and expenses and other finances can help them work out the money part of their agreement.

TANYA

As I write these words, I'm reminded of a case of a woman named Tanya who asked for my help in determining how much alimony she should get as part of her divorce settlement.

Tanya had been married for more than fifteen years to her husband and had reared their two daughters who were now twelve and fourteen. She had never been employed while she was married, although she had begun taking courses toward getting her Ph.D. Before she was married, she had been a language teacher. After the divorce she planned to go back to graduate school to complete her degree so that she could resume her teaching career. However, she had less than $5,000 of her own with which to do it.

Her husband, who was earning an annual salary of over $150,000, had offered to cover all the costs of their kids (who had already agreed to stay with him) and give her an alimony of $2,000 a month for three years. At first glance Tanya thought that this was a pretty good deal, but then she had some second thoughts, and that's when she decided to come to me. I suggested that we examine her educational costs and monthly expenses to see what she would really need to live on and go to school. We estimated these costs and found that she would need a total of $110,000 ($20,000 for tuition, courses, and books and $90,000 for living expenses for two years. (To be safe, I included $18,000 for federal and state income taxes, assuming Tanya would be taxed on any money she received from her ex-husband Will.)

Will's offer of $2,000 for three years amounted to $72,000 (36 months x $2,000). What Tanya needed was $110,000.

I asked Tanya if Will could afford to pay her $110,000; she said he could. His family had money, and he had plenty of savings.

"Then I think it's fair that he pays you this money for the time you spent taking care of the children," I said.

"I do, too," Tanya replied.

I suggested that she show the tuition expenses and the monthly costs we had worked out to Will to see if he would be willing to increase his offer. Tanya wanted me to negotiate for her since she was easily intimidated by him. As she explained it, they had a perfectly friendly relationship, but in money matters he had always assumed control.

I told her I didn't think he would be as receptive to me as

he would be to her, and it would be an important step in establishing her independence to do the negotiating. I reminded her that she would have to be doing it on behalf of her kids so she might as well start now.

I told her I was convinced that once Will saw what she needed, he would be more generous. Since I knew we hadn't overstated Tanya's expenses, I felt that there was no danger of his thinking she was trying to take advantage of him.

After much persuading, Tanya agreed to talk to Will. To her surprise, he was much more receptive than she'd expected. Once he saw her situation and understood that what she was asking for was reasonable, he agreed to pay her a lump sum of $87,000—$15,000 more than his offer. Although this was $23,000 less than the $110,000 she asked for, it was still enough for her to go to school.

As the payment would be considered a property settlement and not alimony, it was not taxable to her. Thus, she would save $18,000 in income taxes, which I had included as a monthly expense. This savings, plus the $5,000 she already had, made up the $23,000 difference.

In telling me about her negotiations, Tanya said that she couldn't have done it without the summary sheet we had worked out. "It was a godsend," she said. "It kept us both grounded."

Divorce negotiations like Tanya's are always ticklish. When parties can anchor their emotions to financial facts, they can often find mutually agreeable solutions to their money problems. Usually, in these cases, an important healing takes place.

The sad part of this story is that the healing occurred at the end of a relationship instead of at the beginning. In my classes I tell students that before they decide to live with anyone, they ought to exchange financial summaries and discuss how they manage their money. This will give them a chance to work out their money problems before they turn into major issues.

I discovered the efficacy of doing this when a young woman named Kimberly wanted me to counsel her and her future husband, Randy, on their finances. Kimberly was concerned because they had such different attitudes.

When they came into my office, I could tell by their appearance that there might be some major differences. Kimberly was dressed in a business coat and skirt, with her hair tied up carefully in a neat bow. Randy was in casual jeans and shirt and had long, flowing hair.

We talked about how they were brought up with money, and Kimberly said that her mother had always lived in constant fear of not having enough although she always seemed to have plenty. She was very tight about spending money and rarely bought anything for herself. I asked Kimberly if she had inherited her traits from her mother, and she said she had.

Randy, on the other hand, admitted he was influenced by his father who never had a dime but could always get money when he wanted it. His father never worried about money and spent more than he had.

I suggested that it might be helpful if I drew up financial summaries for both of them so that they could compare them, and they agreed. I made up two columns on my summary form and wrote down the list of facts.

Whereas Kimberly had $800 in savings and $100,000 in her home, car, and possessions, Randy had only a minus $500 balance in his checkbook and $6,000 in a car and his possessions.

Kimberly had $80,000 in a mortgage and debts; Randy had $10,000 in loans.

On the other hand, in comparing monthly income and expenses, Randy made $3,000 and Kimberly only $1,600. Yet Kimberly showed a savings per month of about $100, while Randy showed he was overspending by approximately $600 per month.

As we discussed these figures, I could see that Kimberly

was obviously the better manager, but she was so tight with her money she rarely had any fun with it. Conversely Randy had no discipline in handling money, but he enjoyed the money he had. In evaluating their attitudes, I saw how they could help each other.

I suggested that they have a joint checking account and each put in a major portion of their incomes into it. The account would be used for all their joint expenses and debts. Since Kimberly was the better manager, I suggested that she take care of the account. However, she couldn't spend money from it unless Randy agreed.

I advised Kimberly to let Randy help her loosen up on her spending. Every month she should buy something that would give her pleasure. I asked Randy to use Kimberly to help him bring some discipline to his money habits. As a start, he might try to put a small amount of his income into a savings account each month.

I advised them not to try to force each other to drastically change their habits since it would only create issues between them. They would be much happier if they accepted their differences and lived with them. I laughed and said that working with the money in their joint checking account would be their therapy!

Kimberly and Randy agreed to follow my advice, and I could tell from their enthusiasm that our session had created a more cooperative spirit between them. As they drove out of my driveway, I wondered how two such opposites could be attracted to each other. "Ah, that's love," was all I could say.

* * *

Exercises:

1. Write down a simple summary of your income and expenses following the directions on page 231.

2. Compare your expenses and adjust your spending to fit your highest priorities. In doing this, consider the psychological and spiritual implications of how you are spending your money.

3. To help control your spending, set yourself a spending goal based on your monthly income, and pencil it in next to your bank balance.

    Subtract the money you spend during the month from your goal, including check payments, PIN or instant card payments, and credit card purchases. Monitor your spending and adjust your expenses to live within your goal.

14

Making the Money
and Spirit Connection

Total Finances

"KNOW THYSELF" is the dictum I use when I'm trying to persuade people to look at their total financial picture. I taught myself how to do this in one of my first cases—which was nearly a fiasco.

A couple, named Kirby and Sandra, came to see me because they were both considering changing their jobs. Kirby was a computer salesman and wanted to buy a computer franchise. Sandra, a kindergarten teacher, was thinking of opening a preschool in her home. They had moved from New York the year before and, now that they felt settled in their new surroundings, were eager to go in different job directions.

Though I wasn't sure how to help them make this decision, I knew that I needed to get an understanding of their financial position, so I began trying to get a picture of their personal finances—savings, debts, monthly income, expenses, etc. The process was slow as both Kirby and Sandra had lots of anxiety and few record-keeping skills. For two-and-a-half hours we struggled to get their financial facts on paper. When I finally thought that I had seen all of them, I was relieved to find that they had enough money to start their ventures.

However, just as the couple was getting ready to leave, Sandra let out a shriek and exclaimed, "Oh, I almost forgot. We still have a mortgage on our house in New York which we're paying off."

"How large is the mortgage?" I asked.

"About $40,000," Sandra replied.

"What are your monthly payments?"

"They run $425 per month."

I was crestfallen by this new information since it completely changed their financial picture and my thinking about their plans. I told them I'd have to reexamine their facts, and—to be sure they didn't miss any—I would draw up a financial summary form they could fill in. We agreed to meet in a week, and I promised to get them the summary in a couple of days.

I went to the library to research financial statements. I found none that was simple enough to use. After many drafts, I finally came up with a one-page summary that I thought had all the information the couple needed. It included their money and property, debts, monthly income, and expenses (see summary on page 237).

I gave Kirby and Sandra the form and had them fill it in. In our next session we reviewed it, and we all agreed that they couldn't afford to leave their jobs until they had sold their place in New York. Although disappointed by the delay, they were relieved not to be going into their ventures too soon.

After they left, I went over the case again and realized my summary had provided the perfect blueprint for working out Kirby and Sandra's money issues. Before they came to me, they were full of self-doubts about their finances, but as soon as they examined their summary, they had new confidence in their ability to cope.

From then on I incorporated the summary in almost all my counseling and teaching, and it has proven itself useful in many ways.

The summary lays out one's financial picture so that anyone can understand it. Many people like Kirby and Sandra have a hard time making sense of their personal finances. By using a one-page form that includes all the essential facts I make this task much easier. Using the summary as a guide, people are able to pull their finances together into a meaningful whole, and once they see them in their totality, the process of managing them becomes much less overwhelming.

The summary also helps people get their money anxieties into perspective. I remember a couple who came to me because the wife was terrified that her husband was overusing their credit cards. They filled in their summary and discovered that though their credit card loans were high, they had more than enough income to cover their monthly loan payments and the rest of their monthly expenses. Once the woman saw this, her fears subsided and she was able to be more accepting of her husband's use of their cards. In this conciliatory atmosphere, the two could then work out a plan to control their debt.

In most cases I discover that after people understand their financial situation, they are much less fearful of it and much more inclined to deal with it. As one person said, "Just thinking about my money paralyzes me, but seeing it on paper makes it manageable."

When people's anxieties about managing have subsided, the summary becomes an invaluable tool for solving their financial problems. With their total picture to guide them, people can easily determine how much they can afford to save and spend, and how they can best change their finances to improve their position or work out their difficulties. *In my twenty-odd years of counseling, I have never found anyone who in examining the summary didn't find some way to improve his or her position.*

Aside from helping people with their money fears and practical problems, the summary provides a meaningful look at their material life, as the picture of their money and property, debts, and monthly income and expenses accurately measures what they have valued.

I had one woman look at her financial picture and burst into tears. I asked her why she was crying, and she said that she was ashamed at how she had been spending her money. This woman had just been diagnosed as having cancer, and I knew that she was looking for ways to heal herself. When she saw how much she had borrowed and spent on her personal pleasures—clothes, dining out, parties, and entertainment—and how little she spent on things that now mattered to her—therapy, massage, nutrition, workshops, and giving to her children—she was full of remorse.

I told her that she hadn't been wasting her money. Up to now she had been spending her resources on what she thought was important. Now she realized she had other priorities. I asked her not to judge her summary but to learn from it, and let it be a tool for guiding her in her new direction.

She took my advice and set up a budget with her new priorities. Knowing that it is always difficult to change one's spending habits, I asked her to keep track of her expenses for several months or until she was sure she was spending the way she wanted to.

When I last heard from her, she was in remission and still living within the budget she had worked out with me. In this case her budget became part of her health program.

Whenever I discuss the healing effects of using my summary, I always emphasize its role in helping people communicate their financial concerns to others. Sharing one's financial situation usually relieves stress and gives one a better perspective on the extent of one's problems. However, most people have trouble doing it. Usually they are afraid of having to reveal themselves because they don't know how to express their position clearly.

Filling in the summary helps people gain the confidence they need to express themselves. It gives them the facts they need. Although they may still feel anxious about revealing these facts to others, they're not nearly as intimidated as when they didn't have this information organized in a meaningful way.

When I am conducting a group meeting, I always tell people that no one is really interested in other people's finances. All they are concerned about is taking care of their own. If they are willing to share the facts of the situations, then other people can help them. I ask people to share only as much as they want to, and if they can talk only about their general issues and not their figures, that is fine. Usually, when people start speaking about their summaries, they lose their fears as they find out that everyone is struggling with similar concerns.

Once I took fourteen hospital employees through this sharing session. When they had just completed their summaries, I turned to an older woman and asked her to begin. There was dead silence, and I could see that everyone was a little uncomfortable.

After a few moments the woman began. She explained how her husband was a truck driver who had just been laid off and how she was struggling with her budget. As she talked, the tension eased as others got caught up in the woman's story. When she ended, people in the group offered sympathy and advice. In the next two hours the group members opened their hearts to each other. Everyone came out of the session feeling uplifted by the experience. They all said it was the first time they had ever had a chance to openly discuss their money concerns.

Besides group sharing, the summary is particularly useful when people are trying to explain their positions in negotiations.

I had one case in which a man was afraid to ask his ex-wife about reducing his alimony payments. After he drew up his summary, he found the courage to make his case because he saw that he couldn't afford both the mortgage on her house and her monthly alimony.

He asked her if she would accept a lower alimony, and she initially refused. However, he showed her his financial summary, and once she realized that his expenses were legitimate and that he couldn't afford the two payments, she agreed to his request.

When I talk to young people, I suggest that before they consider living with a partner or getting married, they exchange summaries so that they can see each other's financial position. Then, if they see any money issues, they can deal with them before they get too involved.

Whether people are living together, marrying, changing jobs, having children, divorcing, retiring, or going through other major life changes, the summary is of great assistance in determining how best to financially plan for it. With a summary of their facts before them, people can see what they have to do to expedite the change.

The most exciting part for me in using the summary is to see how it can transform people's money consciousness. As I help people connect their spirit to their finances on the summary, I see their fears of managing recede and a new confidence take over. They no longer feel intimidated by their finances as they discover that there are psychological, spiritual, and practical ways of mastering them that don't involve more than they can do.

With this new-found confidence, they are much less

negative about managing money and more open to recognizing the psychological and spiritual consequences of their decision making. As people wrestle with their larger money issues, I let the summary of their facts and their intuition be their guide, and I'm always amazed at how the two unerringly help them find the right solutions.

One man told me that in analyzing his summary he resolved not only his financial concern, but some totally unrelated psychological problem he thought he had resolved in past therapy.

His neurosis began when he found out from his tax accountant that he owed over $2,000 in income taxes, which he never expected he'd have to pay. He called me in a panic, and I helped him draw up his summary and work out the best way to meet his payment.

Later on when I saw him, he told me that his money crisis had brought up through his dreams many anxious feelings regarding his mother that seemed unrelated to his tax trauma. He was surprised that these feelings came up since he thought he had worked through them in therapy many years ago, and they hadn't returned until this tax incident. Once his tax problem was solved, he no longer had the dreams or the feelings.

We agreed that his feelings of inadequacy in facing his tax dilemma had triggered his dreams, and finding his solution through his summary analysis had caused them to stop. Before this case I hadn't considered my summary as being such a therapeutic tool. Now I can see how it might be, since it helps people work through many basic anxieties.

Once people like this man are freed from their fears about managing money, many find they would be much happier simplifying their lives and getting rid of unnecessary possessions and property. The summary helps them find ways of living with less money and less stress.

A man who inherited over $2 million discovered this after he built his dream home. From the outset of his project,

I didn't think he could manage the finances of it, but I couldn't get him to stop it, until I had him look at his financial picture a year after the project was completed.

His figures told him that he could afford neither the house nor the life style. He had spent so much money that if he continued, he would have very little of his fortune left. This realization forced him to assess his true feelings about how he was living, and he came to the conclusion that he wasn't happy being tied down to material things, even his dream house. As he said to me, he was a "free spirit."

He had always wanted to live "on the beach," so he decided to sell his home and move to the shores of South America. I'm not sure he would have had the courage to make this change if his financial picture had not shown him how he was wasting away his money and his life.

Even if we don't feel we need to make a major life-style change, I think we all need more time in our lives to savor our family, friends, hobbies, and interests. But most of us give so much time to our money concerns that we never have enough time for these other needs. Examining our summary gives us a chance to work through our money anxieties and free ourselves from their addictive demands.

I shared many of these ideas with Maria as we went through our sessions. Knowing she had little money, no property, no debts, and few possessions, I decided it would be easy to complete her summary after she had filled in her income and expenses.

MARIA'S FINAL SESSION

Since this session was a short one, I have summarized it.

Maria came in with her income and expenses filled in. From these facts plus some cost estimates we made for her tuition, books, and living expenses, we thought that she would need $12,000 from her father for the schooling she needed.

I suggested that she ask him for a $12,000 loan at 8% interest, which she would promise to pay back in monthly installments over five years once she started earning money after her schooling. We looked at a loan payment table and estimated that Maria's monthly loan payments would be about $250.

We incorporated this payment into her projected income and expenses once she completed her courses and began working. She estimated that she could make over $1,500 a month once she had her certificate, an amount which she felt was more than enough to afford the payments.

She was nervous about making this proposal to her father, but I assured her it was worth a try. Knowing that her father was very businesslike, I advised Maria to show him the summary and the calculations we had made.

Our meeting ended with her agreeing that she would call me after she had spoken with her father.

* * *

Several days later Maria called and joyously told me that her father was so impressed with the proposal that he was willing to *give* her the money and call it a loan against her future inheritance.

"I couldn't believe it," Maria said. "He doesn't even like what I want to do."

"I know, but despite all your differences, he's your father, and he loves you," I replied.

There was a pause, and I knew Maria was thinking about what I had said.

"Yes, I guess he does," she said, and there was awe in her tone.

"I'm not surprised," I said. "You made the money and spirit connection we've been talking about."

"How?" Maria asked.

"You gave him a sound financial proposition he could

have confidence in and that opened his heart to be generous with you. Once he knew you could manage your money, he had no qualms about giving you what you needed."

"You mean I had to prove myself first?"

"Yes. I think we all have to prove our ability to manage money before we can get the prosperity we want."

"So I passed the test," Maria said with a laugh.

"You certainly did," I replied. "Now you're on your own. Good luck."

*   *   *

What Maria discovered and what we all need to discover is that love provides the ultimate solution to our money concerns since it is the ultimate force for peace and harmony.

Edgar Cayce said that we should set our ideals and live by them. If you follow the ideals set up for your finances in the titles of chapters 3 to 14, and . . .

Practice Self-Control when you manage your cash;

Find the Right Balance in handling your checking account;

Preserve Yourself by creating meaningful savings and investments;

Value Yourself as you strive to earn money;

Maintain Your Center in the throes of determining how much you spend on your home;

Further Your Journey by dealing realistically with your car costs;

Simplify Your Life by letting go of unnecessary possessions;

Meet Your Commitments when you borrow or lend money;

Find the Right Protection in selecting your insurance;

Share the Burden of taxes by paying your fair amount;

Choose Your Priorities in spending your income; and
Make the Money and Spirit Connection by linking together your finances to your true self . . .

Then you will be well on your way to making that ultimate connection. To follow these ideals, you will find it useful to do the exercises at the end of the chapters. You may want to fill in your summary first to see which ideals need to be worked on.

Now that you have seen how Maria and others made the spiritual connection with money and sorted out their problems, it is your turn to do the same. The peace of mind you will get from following the exercises will make it worth every bit of your effort. You know it's time you got over your anxieties about managing money. They've impeded you long enough. Here is your chance to put them to rest. Please take it.

* * *

Exercises:

1. Fill in your financial summary.

    Make a copy of the financial summary form on p. 237 and fill it in with your own financial facts using the following directions:

    GENERAL DIRECTIONS: In drawing up this summary, keep in mind that your object is to get a meaningful estimate of your current financial picture and that it's more important to get the facts on paper than it is to have them exact. You can always adjust the amounts as you go along.

    Do your summary in pencil so that you can make changes easily.

    Write down amounts to the nearest dollar.

    Put down all your income and expenses on a MONTHLY BASIS.

    When necessary, total the expense for the year and divide by 12. For example, in calculating home insurance, total the quarterly or semi-annual payments and divide by 12. DON'T FORGET TO MAKE THE DIVISION. Otherwise, it badly distorts the expense on the summary.

    In doing your addition, use a calculator with a tape if possible.

    Double-check your figures and your calculations.

    Remember to include every item. It's easy to forget an item when you don't want to look at it. Before writing down your facts, release your judgments about them. Then make sure you put in all of them.

Now you are ready. Let's go through the instructions for writing down each item on the summary.

Instructions for Filling in the Summary

Cash Write down the amount you have on hand, including any funds in jars, envelopes, under the mattress, etc.

Checking Account Write down the total amount in all regular checking accounts. Do not include money in money market fund checking accounts or mutual fund checking accounts.

Savings Account Write down the total amount in all regular savings accounts (usually paying 5% to 5 1/2% interest). Do not include money in C.D.s or other investments.

Investments Write down the total market value of your intangible investments, including C.D.s, money market funds, stocks, bonds, annuities, etc. Include all investments in retirement plans. If you have trouble calculating your investments, read number 4 on p. 64.

Take a sub-total of your available funds.

Home Write down a reasonable estimate of the market value of your home. A local real estate agent can give you an estimate.

Other Properties Write down the market value of all other properties, including land, buildings, business, partnerships, cash surrender value of insurance, etc.

Personal Possessions Write down an approximate value of

all your personal possessions, including clothes, furniture, antiques, art, computers, VCRs, TVs, etc. You can use these ranges—$1,000-$4,000; $5,000-$7,000, $8,000-$10,000 on up. You just need a good guess here.

Cars/Vehicles Write down the market value of your car(s) or other vehicle(s). Note: You may want to get this estimate from your dealer.

Take a sub-total of your properties.

Take a total of your money and property.

Money owed to you Write down any loans owed to you.

Bills Write down any bills outstanding for more than thirty days. Note: Do not include credit card loans.

Loans (owed to others) Write down any loans owed to others, including personal loans, credit card loans, business loans, second mortgages, etc.

Mortgage Write down the outstanding balance on your mortgage.

Take a total of all your debts.

Income List your MONTHLY income from all sources. Remember to put in the amount on a monthly basis, i.e., divide the annual income by 12. Include income from salaries (gross and net), business, investments, partnerships, gifts, and sales (if ongoing).

Monthly Expenses

Some people have trouble estimating their expenses, especially their entertainment, clothes, and gifts. If you will take a few moments and review the amounts after you have calculated them, your intuition will tell you if your estimates are reasonable. I've learned through many consultations that the subconscious mind knows your spending habits, and with a little work you can come up with the amount that feels right.

Mortgage or Rent Write down your monthly mortgage payment or your rent.

Utilities Write down your heat, water, sewer, and trash. Do not include telephone.

Maintenance Write down any costs for maintaining your home, including roofing, plumbing, electrical service, cleaning, landscaping, furnitures, fixtures, etc. Try to estimate the coming year's needs. Calculate a MONTHLY amount.

Telephone Write down an average monthly estimate of your telephone bill.

Food Write down the amount you spend on basic food supplies, including household basics.

Loan Payments Write down your total monthly loan payments. You may want to put your car loan payment under travel costs to identify the cost of your car.

Clothes Write down the estimated amount you spend on clothes. Add up your annual shopping and divide by 12 to get a monthly amount. Note: It may help to review your seasonal shopping habits.

Car and Travel Write down all your car costs—gas, insurance, maintenance. You may want to include your car loan payment(s) just to see how much you spend on your car(s). If you do, do not add that amount to your monthly loan payments. Also include any regular travel costs (not including vacations which are discretionary).

Medical Write down the monthly costs of medical insurance, the cost of your share of medical expenses, dental expenses, therapy, and any other medical costs. Do not include medical insurance deducted from your paycheck.

Personal Care Write down monthly expenses of personal care items, such as hair cuts, laundry, vitamins, massage, dry cleaning, etc.

Entertainment Write down monthly amounts for entertainment. These include all restaurant and bar costs, movies, videos, clubs, camping, weekends away (not vacations), theater, skiing, other athletics, music lessons, hobbies, etc.

Education Write down all your educational costs, including tuitions, courses, workshops, etc. Create monthly estimates.

Gifts Write down all your gifts, including charitable gifts. You may find it helpful to calculate the number of people you give to for Christmas, birthdays, and other events, and then calculate an average amount for each gift. Be sure to put the total in a monthly amount.

Insurance Write down your monthly expense for home, life, and any other insurance *except* car and health, which you've already included under travel and medical, respectively. Don't include life insurance, if it is deducted from your paycheck, or property insurance, which is part of your mortgage payment.

Taxes Write down a monthly portion of your property taxes and income taxes. Don't include the income taxes that have already been deducted from your paycheck or property taxes that are included as part of your mortgage payment.

Vacation Write down a monthly estimate for your vacation expense.

Other Write down a total for monthly expenses in other categories, including publications, animals, postage, tax and finance service, maid service, garden, children's allowances, and business (assuming you haven't included a net income amount under MONEY RECEIVED DURING MONTH).

Miscellaneous Write down an estimate for unaccounted-for items.

Take a total of your monthly expenses.

This completes your financial summary.

Exercise 2. Examine your cash, checking account, savings, and investments and follow the ideals and exercises in chapters 3 to 5.

Exercise 3. Examine the value of your home (if you own one), properties, possessions, and car. Follow the ideals and exercises in chapters 7 to 9.

Exercise 4. Examine your debts and follow the ideals and exercises in chapters 7 and 10.

Exercise 5. Compare your monthly income to your monthly expenses. If you are overspending, see how you can get them in balance. Follow the ideals and exercises in chapters 6, 7, 8, 10, 11, 12, and 13.

Exercise 6.   Examine your total financial summary and decide what you need to do to improve your position, solve money problems, plan life changes, and manage your money with greater confidence and care. Note: Refer to chapter 14.

*   *   *

Financial Summary

MONEY AND PROPERTY

Cash	_____
Checking Account	_____
Savings Account	_____
Investments	_____
Sub-total	_____
Home	_____
Other Properties	_____
Personal Possessions	_____
Car(s)/Vehicles	_____
Sub-total	_____
Grand Total	_____

MONEY OWED TO YOU

Loans	_____

MONEY OWED TO OTHERS

Bills	_____
Loans	_____
Mortgage	_____
Total Loans	_____

MONEY RECEIVED DURING MONTH

Paycheck(s) Gross	_____
Net	_____
Retirement Benefit	_____
Income from Investments	_____
Other Income	_____
Sub-total	_____
Sales of Properties	_____
Gifts	_____
Total Money Received	_____

MONEY SPENT DURING MONTH

Mortgage or Rent	_____
Utilities	_____
Maintenance	_____
Telephone	_____
Food	_____
Loan Payments	_____
Clothes	_____
Car and Travel	_____
Medical	_____
Personal Care	_____
Entertainment	_____
Education	_____
Gifts	_____
Insurance	_____
Taxes	_____
Vacation	_____
Other	_____
	_____
	_____
	_____
	_____
	_____
Miscellaneous	_____
Total Expenses	_____

Endnotes

1. For more information on Edgar Cayce you may want to read *There Is a River* by Thomas Sugrue (New York, N.Y.: Holt, Rinehart and Winston, 1942).

2. Roberts, Jane. *The Nature of Personal Reality.* New York, N.Y.: Bantam Books, 1978.

3. To get a better understanding of Cayce's ideas, you may want to read *Think on These Things* (Virginia Beach, Va.: A.R.E. Press, 1981).

4. Goldberg, Elliot, ed. *Inner Balance: The Power of Holistic Healing.* Selye, Hans. "Self-Regulation: The Response to Stress." Englewood Cliffs, N.J.: Prentice-Hall, Inc., 1979, p. 66.

5. There are many meanings to karma. Here I'm using karma to mean sacred work.

6. *Bhagavad Gita.* New York, N.Y.: Penguin Classics, 1962, p. 67, verse 12.

7. Allen, James. *As a Man Thinketh.* Marina del Rey, Calif.: DeVorss & Company, p. 50.

8. Rodegast and Stanton. *Emmanuel's Book.* New York, N.Y.: Some Friends of Emmanuel, 1985, p. 116.

9. Easwaran, Eknath. *Meditation.* Tomales, Calif.: Nilgiri Press, 1978.

10. Cayce, Edgar. *Think on These Things. Op cit.,* reading 1971-1, p. 78.

11. Rodegast and Stanton. *Op. cit.,* p. 128.

12. Roman and Packer. *Creating Money.* Tiburon, Calif.: H.J. Kramer, Inc., 1988, p. 103.

13. *Ibid.*

14. Ponder, Catherine. *The Healing Secrets of the Ages.* New York, N.Y.: Parker Publishing, 1981.

15. Moore, Thomas. *Care of the Soul.* New York, N.Y.: HarperCollins, 1992, p. 193.

16. Dass and Gorman. *How Can I Help?* New York, N.Y.: Alfred A. Knopf, 1985, p. 236.

17 Hanh, Thich Nhat. *Touching Peace* (1992) and *Being Peace* (1990). Berkeley, Calif.: Parallax Press.

18. *Ibid., Being Peace.*

19. Hanh, *Touching Peace. Op. cit.,* p. 25.

About the Author

Frederick S. Brown's background includes a B.A. degree from Yale, course work at the New York Institute and the Wharton Business School, ten years as a stockbroker, eleven years as an investment advisor, and more than twenty years as a personal financial consultant and writer. His published works include four personal finance books and articles for various newspapers and magazines. In addition, Mr. Brown has been giving workshops on money management for over fifteen years.

What Is A.R.E.?

The Association for Research and Enlightenment, Inc. (A.R.E.®), is the international headquarters for the work of Edgar Cayce (1877-1945), who is considered the best-documented psychic of the twentieth century. Founded in 1931, the A.R.E. consists of a community of people from all walks of life and spiritual traditions, who have found meaningful and life-transformative insights from the readings of Edgar Cayce.

Although A.R.E. headquarters is located in Virginia Beach, Virginia—where visitors are always welcome—the A.R.E. community is a global network of individuals who offer conferences, educational activities, and fellowship around the world. People of every age are invited to participate in programs that focus on such topics as holistic health, dreams, reincarnation, ESP, the power of the mind, meditation, and personal spirituality.

In addition to study groups and various activities, the A.R.E. offers membership benefits and services, a bimonthly magazine, a newsletter, extracts from the Cayce readings, conferences, international tours, a massage school curriculum, an impressive volunteer network, a retreat-type camp for children and adults, and A.R.E. contacts around the world. A.R.E. also maintains an affiliation with Atlantic University, which offers a master's degree program in Transpersonal Studies.

For additional information about A.R.E. activities hosted near you, please contact:

A.R.E.
67th St. and Atlantic Ave.
P.O. Box 595
Virginia Beach, VA 23451-0595
(804) 428-3588

A.R.E. Press

A.R.E. Press is a publisher and distributor of books, audiotapes, and videos that offer guidance for a more fulfilling life. Our products are based on, or are compatible with, the concepts in the psychic readings of Edgar Cayce.

We especially seek to create products which carry forward the inspirational story of individuals who have made practical application of the Cayce legacy.

For a free catalog, please write to A.R.E. Press at the address below or call toll free 1-800-723-1112. For any other information, please call 804-428-3588.

A.R.E. Press
Sixty-Eighth & Atlantic Avenue
P.O. Box 656
Virginia Beach, VA 23451-0656